Multimodal Literacy

RESEARCHING
CLASSROOM
PRACTICE

MAUREEN WALSH

Evelyn,
Hope you find this interesting
- explains why my 'other' writing
has been slow!
Best to you, Maureen & Julie -
Maureen xxx

e:lit
**Primary
English
Teaching
Association**

expertise in primary literacies

First published 2011
Primary English Teaching Association (e:lit)
Laura St Newtown NSW 2042 Australia
PO Box 3106 Marrickville Metro NSW 2204
Tel: (02) 9565 1277
Fax: (02) 9565 1070
Email: info@elit.edu.au
Website: www.elit.edu.au

ISBN: 978-1-875622-82-5

National Library of Australia Cataloguing-in-Publication entry
    Walsh, Maureen
    Multimodal literacy : classroom research and practice
    Edition: 1st ed
    ISBN: 9781875622825 (pbk.)
    Notes: Includes bibliographical references.
    Subjects: Critical pedagogy / Literacy
    Dewey Number: 370.115

Cover and internal design by Avril Makula
Edited by Rema Gnanadickam, Zodiac Publishing Services
Printed in Australia by Ligare Pty Ltd

This book has been printed on paper certified
by the Program for the Endorsement of Forest
Chain of Custody (PEFC). PEFC is committed
to sustainable forest management through third
party forest certification managed forests.

CONTENTS

ACKNOWLEDGMENTS

There are many acknowledgements to be made to people whose work has contributed to this book in some way. The collaboration between Australian Catholic University and the Catholic Education Office (CEO) Sydney has allowed this research to evolve over several years.

I would particularly like to thank: Seamus O'Grady, Director of Curriculum and Dr Kate O'Brien, Head of Primary for their support; and to others at CEO Sydney: Diane Brook, Helen Christou, Sue Sinko and the earlier commitment of Kate Clancy (now Principal, Santa Sabina College).

I thank Michelle Tamaro and Jennifer Asha for their invaluable research assistance.

The classroom examples explored in this book are taken from the *Multimodal Literacy Project Reports*, 2008 and 2009.

I wish to express my appreciation to the Principals who allowed this research to occur in their schools and to all the 50 teachers and many students who participated in this research. Special thanks go to the following teachers whose work is included in this book: Nicole Kolibac, Romina DeGrazia, Mandi Gahan, Diane Hunt, Zeina Chalich, Margarita Caamano, Rebekka Rukker, Maree Rooke, Maureen Burns, David Neilson, Andrew Tate, Itziar Hutchinson, Emma Booth, Lauren Magnus, Kimberley Keys, Rearne Goodwin, George Bounas, Alfina Pappalardo, Gae Flood, Cathy Cooper, Judith Callaghan, Catherine Branley, Alison Bonnano, Monica Hallinan, Angela Anders, Nicole Young, Nicole Pierce, Sean Brown, Angela Chisari, Carmela Porreca, Jenni McCrindle, Catherine Liu, Nicale Tleige, Lauren O'Neill, Nadia Eichwald, Jessica Roche, Lisa Duggan, Linda Thomas, Mariella Buttigieg, Alic Gobeli, Trish Guigni, Peter Kelahar, Chad Ferris and Mary Harb.

Maureen Walsh

FOREWORD

At the close of the first decade of the new millennium, we know much more about young children's engagement with a range of digital and multimodal texts from birth. There is a rich range of research that outlines how children navigate a range of media and modes in their meaning-making practices outside of school. However, we still lack in-depth analyses of multimodal text analysis and production in primary classrooms. This book, therefore, is important in that it provides a range of insights, using case studies of innovative practices in classrooms, into approaches to curricula and pedagogy in a digital age. The rich examples of children's work are located within detailed accounts of the context of their production, which enables a fuller understanding of how to foster children's skills, knowledge and understanding in relation to the analysis and production of multimodal, multimedia texts. A breathtaking range of texts is included in these pages, from videos and digital books to comics, blogs and wikis. The way in which the affordances of new media enable collaborative approaches to reading and writing is highlighted and the implications for children's engagement in a participatory culture reflected upon. Furthermore, the outline of classroom practice is underpinned by a clear account of the theoretical framework for this work. Challenging concepts are explained clearly and illustrated through helpful diagrams and classroom examples, offering a praxis of multimodality. The author cuts a clear path across the complex landscape of contemporary communication and highlights the key features of this new and exciting terrain. By the end of this book, readers will have a fuller understanding of the nature of teaching and learning in a digital age. The account is not simply celebratory, however. Exciting though it is to be presented with such innovative accounts of classroom practice, the author does outline the challenges to be faced; she does not shy away from asking searching questions about the nature of assessment, or the relationship between traditional, print-based literacy skills and the 'new basics' of multimodal, multimedia text analysis and production. These are the key questions which will face us in the decades ahead and they are questions which will require rigorous, research-based accounts of pioneering classroom practice in which teachers and academics collaborate in the investigation of significant pedagogical and curricula issues. This book provides a model for that work and highlights how, through respectful and reflective approaches to classroom-based research, we can work across traditional professional boundaries in the pursuit of new knowledge. We can be certain that, in the years ahead, children will move ever more steadily into a world in which the reading and writing of multimodal, multimedia texts is dependent upon a set of skills and knowledge that we are only just in the process of working out. At a time when we lack considered accounts of multimodality in practice, this book provides a solid grounding for future explorations and sets out a clear agenda for action. As the author suggests, we need to move beyond the "new" of "new literacies" if we are to develop classroom curricula and pedagogy fitting for the 21st century and this text does just that – thus, in itself, offering a "new" and exciting approach to accounts of multimodal classroom practice.

Jackie Marsh,
Professor and Head of The School of Education
and The Department of Educational Studies
University of Sheffield, October 2010

Introduction

NEW MEANS OF COMMUNICATION: WHEN DOES THE 'NEW' END?

From the time of writing this book to the time when it has been published, there will have been changes in digital communications technology. These changes inevitably impact on the literacy practices of students at home and at school. Technological changes have always impacted on human communication and contributed to social change, however the impact of digital technologies in the 21st century has been unprecedented. Coiro et al (2008) aptly sum up this impact:

> No previous technology for literacy has been adopted by so many, in so many different places, in such a short period, and with such profound consequences. No previous technology for literacy permits the immediate dissemination of even newer technologies of literacy to every person on the Internet by connecting to a single link on a screen. (pp.2–3)

At the moment we are able to communicate instantly with combinations of text, photos or videos through mobile phone technology, different types of computers and multimedia devices, such as the *Kindle*, the *iphone* and the *ipad*, and obtain instant information from the internet using these devices and their applications. With Web 2.0, social changes have accompanied these technological developments. We can participate in twittering, wikis, blogs or various social networking sites (e.g. *MySpace*, *Facebook*, *YouTube*, *Flikr*); or participate in a virtual environment through gaming or in virtual worlds such as *Second Life*. Many such sites are rapidly developing for children (Bebo, ClubPenguin.com, Poptropica.com, FreeRealms.com). These communication environments are changing the way people present themselves and the way relationships are developed. We know that new technology is constantly being developed so that smaller and more mobile communication forms will become available. The 'new' of the future is constantly replacing the 'new' of now. We do not know how these continued developments will impact on society but we need to examine what these constant changes mean for literacy education in schools.

Implications of these changes in communication for education have been debated for some time and new theoretical views of literacy have been supported by worldwide research. However the actual transfer of new theories into educational policy and curriculum has been much slower. In Australia we have an Australian Curriculum: English (ACARA, 2010) that includes references to digital texts and multimodal texts, thus acknowledging that students may create these texts as well as read and view them. This acknowledgment needs to be further developed so that the links between new theories of communication and classroom practice are clearly articulated.

THE RESEARCH BASIS OF THIS BOOK

This book provides ideas for such articulation between theory and practice by reporting on ongoing research in real classrooms. For several years the Catholic Education Office, Sydney with the Australian Catholic University has supported this research in its primary schools to examine what the constant changes in communication mean for literacy education in the twenty-first century. The principal aims of the research have been to investigate:

1 the literacy strategies needed for reading, using and producing multimodal texts; and
2 the relevant, explicit pedagogy appropriate for integrating literacy learning within both print-based and digital communication environments.

These aims were linked to goals of professional learning for teachers. Teachers were engaged in new learning by participating in the research. In initial meetings with the researcher they were presented with theories of literacy within new communicative, multimodal environments and encouraged to reflect on the classroom implications of these. They were led to examine the design and structure of multimodal texts. Through the organisation of information sessions about the research, teachers understood the aims of the research and were encouraged to engage in reflective practice through their planning and observations of student learning. Samples of teachers' reflections and students' comments are provided through this book to show the impact of the research on the teachers and on student learning.

This research has been occurring in primary schools in metropolitan Sydney over the last five years. In this book, for ease of organisation and currency, the main aspects of research referred to will be the classroom data that was analysed in 2008 and 2009. Sixteen teachers from six Catholic Primary Schools (Kindergarten to Year 6) participated in the research in 2008 and thirty-four teachers from seventeen Primary schools in 2009. Many of the schools had large numbers of second language learners of English. Teachers volunteered for participation in the research in response to an invitation from their employing authority. They were selected on the basis of their interest and experience, particularly their interest in investigating new pedagogy for literacy. Teachers worked within teams, usually of two or three, and developed integrated programs across different curriculum areas, combining print and digital texts for students' engagement in reading, responding to, viewing, writing and producing texts.

Methodology

The study used a mixed method design with online questionnaires and multiple case studies. The online questionnaires were designed to obtain information about students' use of the internet and digital texts, as well as print-based texts, outside school. Questionnaires were completed by teachers at the beginning and end of each year. The qualitative design of the study was an incorporation of professional learning and research. Teachers worked with the researcher within the paradigm of collaborative participatory research (Wagner, 1997, pp. 13–22; Yelland, Lee, O'Rourke & Harrison, 2008, p.16). This approach to research maintains a balance between developing new knowledge and involving the members of the community with the teachers as partners in the research. The researcher developed the survey and completed classroom observations and analysis of data aided by research assistants and curriculum advisers.

Teachers planned their program and kept diaries with notes on their classroom observations. They submitted these diaries and a written report along with samples of students' work in print and digital form. Data consisted of classroom observations, diaries in photo and video files; teachers' programs, reports and reflections; samples of students' work in print and digital mode, and students' comments on their learning. Guidelines were developed for observations of specific aspects of students' literacy behaviour. The data was analysed to discern common themes related to specific aspects of language and literacy learning. In the first instance students' work was separated into outcomes and indicators from the *NSW K-6 English Syllabus* of talking and listening, reading, viewing and writing. Each case study was analysed to identify how aspects of digital communication were incorporated into the criteria of talking and listening, reading and viewing, and writing.

The results of the research provide specific examples of ways in which teachers and students were engaging with digital communication for language and literacy learning and shaping future classroom practice. Detailed findings, methodology and data analysis are discussed in other publications (Walsh, 2008; 2009; 2010). Significant aspects of the findings are presented and discussed in this book.

THE PURPOSE OF THIS BOOK

This book attempts to demonstrate the articulation of theory into classroom research and practice within a conceptual framework of literacy as grounded in social practice (Barton, 1994; Street, 1995). The author acknowledges the research that has occurred in the last two decades on aspects of multliteracies, multimodality, semiotics and new literacies (Cope & Kalantzis, 2001; Kress & van Leeuwen. 1996, 2001; Kress, 2003; 2010; Lankshear & Knobel, 2003; Marsh, 2002; Unsworth, 2001) and builds on these through new classroom research.

No doubt many teachers worldwide are adapting in creative and effective ways to the changes in digital communication. This book does not offer or propose a definitive methodology, nor is it focused on all the facilities or potential of digital technology. Rather it provides snapshots of how several Sydney teachers, with available resources, have adapted to the changes in digital communication to develop appropriate and sustainable pedagogy. The results of the research are shown to provide specific examples of ways in which teachers and students have been engaging with digital communication for literacy learning and shaping future classrooms. The research demonstrates how literacy is multimodal and needs to be re-defined within new communication environments.

This book draws on the theories and research of others and builds on these through classroom research to:
• provide evidence of new literacy practices within print and digital environments
• describe and define these new literacy practices
• present examples of changed pedagogy for literacy learning
• provide teachers with ideas for reflecting on their own literacy teaching practices.

CHAPTER 1

Literacy in a changed communication environment

INTRODUCTION

Recently, as part of our research, we conducted a small survey of primary school students across nine schools to provide information about their activities at home with reading, watching television, gaming, accessing the internet or other digital media. This survey was influenced by the United Kingdom Literacy Association (UKLA) *Reading on Screen Report* (Bearne et al, 2007) which investigated students' literacy activities outside school in order to consider how these activities might be impacting on students' literacy learning in school. The UKLA study found that students of all ages in the primary school showed a preference for choosing 'screen-based texts, particularly popular children's internet sites, over paper-based texts' (p.10). Similar results were found in our Sydney study, showing particular trends with gender differences and younger children rapidly gaining proficiency with digital texts.

Results of responses from the students who ranged across all primary school grades (Kindergarten to Year 6, ages 5–12) are summarised in Table 1, showing a breakdown of students' responses in relation to reading habits, computer gaming, use of the internet, and use of other digital technologies.

These findings reveal that many students were accessing digital technologies at home. The majority of students were not reading books for leisure. The results

TABLE 1. SUMMARY OF QUESTIONNAIRE RESULTS	
READING BOOKS – PRACTICE AND ATTITUDES	• 46% girls, 38% boys in Years 1–2 indicated they enjoyed reading for leisure. By Years 5–6 the responses to this item were 44% girls, 10% boys. • Fewer than 30% of Year 5–6 students read novels at home. • 50% of Year 5–6 boys thought 'reading was boring' compared with 10% of girls.
PLAYING COMPUTER GAMES	• Over 50% of all students preferred playing computer games to reading or watching TV. • 96% of Year 5–6 students selected 'playing computer games' as their preferred spare time activity.
USE OF THE INTERNET AT HOME	• Most of Year 5–6 students indicated they used the internet at home for school projects. • In younger years more girls than boys indicated they used the internet at home for school projects. • In Kindergarten, Years 1 and 2, the majority of boys indicated they used the internet in their spare time for activities not associated with school work
USE OF OTHER DIGITAL TECHNOLOGIES	• 40–90% of all students indicated confidence with using a digital camera. A similar percentage responded in Kindergarten with a higher indication from boys. More than 40% of all students had used Photoshop, media player, and made a podcast. • Responses from younger students suggested they were as familiar as older students with digital photography technology.

are consistent with findings of the UK study and other research (Marsh et al, 2005) that has shown that, outside school, students are more likely to be engaged in activities with digital and mobile technology such as instant messaging, gaming and social networking. Moreover there has been a prevailing argument for some time (Prensky, 2001; Gee 2003) that today's students are learning differently because of the changes in communication and that these differences have impacted on social changes.

....

REFLECTION

• **How do these results compare with your knowledge of students' use of digital technologies at home?**
• **Would you conduct a similar survey with your students?**
• **Do you observe a difference between students' socio-economic backgrounds and access to digital technologies at home?**
• **What are the challenges for ensuring students, particularly in the older grades, still read and enjoy good literature?**

....

There are several implications for educators, particularly the challenge of maintaining students' motivation to continue to read books and to engage in sustained reading of varieties of print-based texts, especially literature. It is evident that many students from a younger age are becoming proficient in the use of a range of digital technologies, which have become available and affordable in the home. Do students from lower SES backgrounds or different cultures have similar access to new technologies at home? Whatever the answer, it is essential that these technologies are available in schools and the Australian Government's 'digital education revolution' policy (DEEWR, 2008) has been endeavouring to ensure that more technology is being supplied to schools throughout the country. It is essential that teachers know how to use new technology effectively within their programs and to use it in ways that enhance students' literacy and learning.

THE NEED FOR A CHANGED PEDAGOGY FOR LITERACY

If, as the survey and associated research confirms, many students are choosing to engage more in new technologies than with books at home, then classroom contexts need to acknowledge these changes. Teachers need to be able to develop pedagogy that embeds digital communication technologies and texts to meet curriculum outcomes and assessment requirements while at the same time maintaining students' engagement with print-based technologies, particularly literature. In order to consider the appropriate changes needed, it is necessary for teachers to understand the nature of the differences in literacy practices with the use of digital technologies. Reading and writing with digital and multimodal texts requires several different processes than reading and writing with print-based texts. Some of these differences are now explained.

READING AND WRITING WITH PRINT-BASED AND MULTIMODAL TEXTS: DIFFERENCES AND SIMILARITIES

Reading and writing are both about making meaning.

When we read we have a purpose, such as enjoying a literary text or gaining new knowledge from an information text. We gain meaning as we decode and interact with a text, linking our background experiences to new experiences or knowledge.

When we write, we write out our thoughts, communicate information, create a story, explain or discuss ideas.

Reading, or writing, does not occur in isolation but usually for a purpose and within a context. Figure 1 represents this process of reading and writing with print-based texts, showing that a social context and social purpose underlie these activities. The diagram highlights the spoken and written 'modes' (Halliday, 1985)

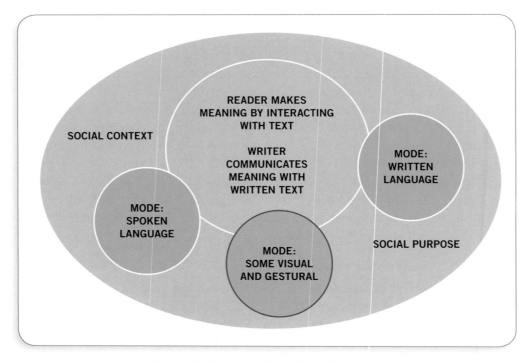

Figure 1. Reading and writing with print-based texts

that occur in reading and writing print-based texts. Mode refers to the means of communication and written texts consist primarily of the modes of spoken language (i.e. spoken language written down) or written language. The diagram also shows that visual and gestural modes (Kress & van Leeuwen, 2001) occur with reading and writing to some extent.

Figure 1 shows that some visual or gestural modes may occur in reading or writing print-based texts. If images or graphics are included in a book, newspaper or magazine these are referred to as visual modes. A print-based text can be 'multimodal' if the reader has to process more than one mode, such as a written text with an illustration or diagram. Even if there are no illustrations or graphics in a text there are of course visual processes that occur as the reader has to see and decode the print, font, layout and punctuation on the page; or for the writer who has to encode and produce written text. There are gestural modes of holding a book, turning a page and writing on a page. However as Kress (2003) and others have shown written language is primarily a linear, sequential process. This process is the way reading and writing have been taught and been assessed in classrooms for decades until recently.

In contrast, reading and writing with screen-based, digital texts entails the reading, viewing and writing of text with images that are usually not presented in

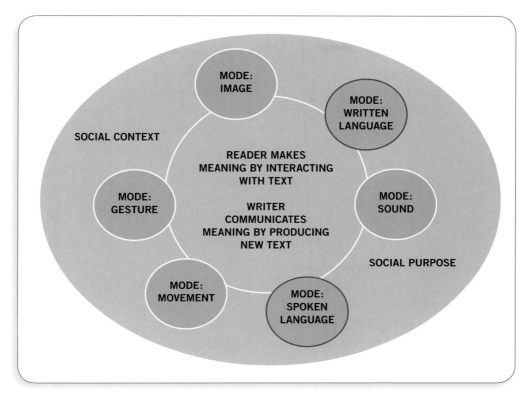

Figure 2. Reading and writing with multimodal and digital texts

a linear format. Other modes that may occur along with written text are image, sound, movement and gesture. Thus the term 'multimodal' has been used in recent years to describe the non-linear production or processing of texts that occur primarily on a screen. Picture books and information books can be multimodal in the way visual and verbal modes are constructed. However, the principal mediums through which multiple modes can occur are film and television, computer screens, interactive white boards, game consoles, mobile phones and various mobile devices such as *Kindle*s or other e-books, *iphone*s or *ipad*s.

Whatever the screen medium there are more modes than with print-based texts that need to be processed so that the distinction between reading and viewing are hard to determine. Similarly a 'writer' can now design and produce a text that combines images and graphics with written text as well as sound and movement on screen. Figure 2 represents this process of reading and writing with multimodal and digital texts.

Reading and writing with multimodal texts is still about making and communicating meaning as with print-based texts. However, the reader or writer is required to process a range of different modes that may occur: text and image in a wordless picture book; or a number of modes such as written text, image, sound and movement in a digital narrative. These aspects of reading and writing on screen entail different processes from the reading, writing and producing of print-based texts and several researchers have demonstrated these differences (Kress, 2003; Snyder, 1997; Lankshear & Knobel, 2003; Unsworth, 2003; Walsh 2006).

The theory of multimodality (Kress & van Leeuwen, 2001; Kress, 2003; 2010) has been the basis for the contention that the simultaneous processing of different modes of text, image, sound and gesture in visual, media or digital texts is a different function from the linear, sequential reading of print-based texts. Other theorists and researchers (Snyder, 1997; Lankshear, Gee, Knobel & Searle, 1997) have supported this view for some time and attempted to theorise the changed nature of literacy within new communication environments.

Further aspects of reading on screen

The navigation of screen-based texts thus involves a process that is quite different from the left-to-right, linear reading of print-based texts. The UKLA study previously referred to (Bearne et al, 2007) provides evidence to show that students, across an age range from three to sixteen, use a range of skills and strategies for reading screen-based texts. Researchers' observations confirmed that students were involved in 'radial browsing'. They were able to trawl language, image and music as well as highlight key sections to retrieve information. While students were able to apply aspects of comprehension to obtain screen-based information it was 'orchestrating the different modes to make meaning' (p.20) that was seen as a different process from the reading of print-based texts.

We need to realise, however, that we cannot just consider the differences between reading print and reading on screen as static comparisons. Reading on screen involves various aspects of online processing that includes responding to animated icons, hypertext, sound effects; and navigating pathways between and within screens. Researchers (Lawless & Shrader, 2008) have only begun to understand the processes of navigating hypermedia along with both the intertexual and intratexual characteristics of cyberspace environments.

Students of today quickly adapt to the navigation potential and the processing of different modes within digital texts. This processing itself often incorporates a merging and synchronising of text, images, sound and movement as these occur in recent digital products, such as the *iPhone* for example. We do not know how such processing and morphing of messages and texts is affecting the way children learn, or if the processes involved in activities such as texting, blogging, or communicating online are developing different cognitive abilities than those required for reading and writing traditional print-based texts. Gee's research (2003) on video gaming suggests that the procedures involved offer cognitive advantages with intricate literacy and learning opportunities. The touch features of recent products such as the *iPhone*, *iTouch* and the *iPad* rely much more on gestural, spatial and kinaesthetic movements that need further investigation as to the way this processing is affecting cognitive processes.

Further aspects of writing on screen

While writing on screen has existed for a long time with word-processing facilities, 'writing' now very often entails assembling a product that may contain written text as well as quite sophisticated layout, graphics, photographs and images, even hypertext. Bearne (2003) has for some time explicated the possibilities of teachers using students' writing and production of multimodal texts within classroom literacy programs. Recently, Bearne & Wolstencroft (2007) have demonstrated ways of teachers programming and assessing writing through students' multimodal texts. They emphasise the interrelationship between reading and writing in producing texts and explain how students need to understand the meaning-making potential of different modes, particularly the relationship between words and images, in reading, writing and producing multimodal texts.

The facilities of Web 2.0 have further changed the possibilities of students' writing and text production. A weblog or blog, for example, is produced with appropriate layout for screen and can combine text, images, graphics, photos or video with sound and music. Design is important for blogs and the design will be carefully developed to reflect the author/producer and to engage the audience who can respond with text and images. For students to produce multimodal texts they need to consider and understand features of design such as layout, composition, use of text and image or graphics – including aspects such as colour, size, medium, angles – and the way these are appropriate for a specific audience. It is significant that other researchers have been investigating design as integral to literacy pedagogy (Kalantzis & Cope, 2005; Healy, 2008).

More than technology

While considering these differences in both reading and writing on screen compared with print-based texts, it is now impossible to see reading and writing as separate. They frequently occur together. Nor is it sensible to separate the technical, functional processes of reading or writing on screen from the social practices that accompany these processes (Carrington, 2005). These social practices of literacy have changed and expanded exponentially with the development of Web 2.0 technology and have many implications for classroom practice that will be considered throughout this book.

Considering the changes that have occurred in reading and writing with multimodal and digital texts, the author has chosen the term 'multimodal literacy' to explain the way reading and writing may be different in classroom contexts where students are using both print and multimodal texts, sometimes separately and sometimes together. While other researchers have used this term (Kress & Jewitt, 2003; Pahl & Rowsell, 2005), it is explained here in the light of classroom applications and the research basis of this book.

MULTIMODAL LITERACY: WHAT DOES IT MEAN?

The term 'multimodal literacy' is used in this book to explain the process of reading, viewing, writing and producing both print and multimodal texts in classroom contexts.

MULTIMODAL LITERACY refers to meaning-making that occurs through the reading, viewing, understanding, responding to, producing and interacting with written text combined with other modes, particularly with screen-based texts. Multimodal literacy may include listening, talking, enacting and investigating as well as writing, designing and producing such texts. The processing of modes, such as image, words, sound, gesture and movement within texts can occur simultaneously and is often cohesive and synchronous. Sometimes specific modes may dominate or converge.

Figure 3 illustrates this process of multimodal literacy as it can occur in classrooms. The diagram shows the merging of the two inner circles to represent the way reading and writing have been extended with digital and multimodal texts while meaning making is still the central core of literacy. Students may be required to read both print and multimodal texts and will therefore be interacting with a variety of modes. Reading and writing are often interrelated, and writing leads to the design and production of a multimodal text or digital product for a specific audience. Figure 3 shows that reading and writing with spoken, print and digital texts are interchangeable resources within classrooms. Making and communicating meaning are still the core purpose of literacy in multimodal classroom contexts. However reading and writing now have the potential to be communicated through and with a variety of modes. Along with the interaction between modes of written texts, image, sound and movement there is often interaction between students in this environment. Oral language is an important factor as students plan, investigate and collaborate on interpreting or producing multimodal texts. Social context and social purpose remain the basis for any type of communication within classroom learning contexts.

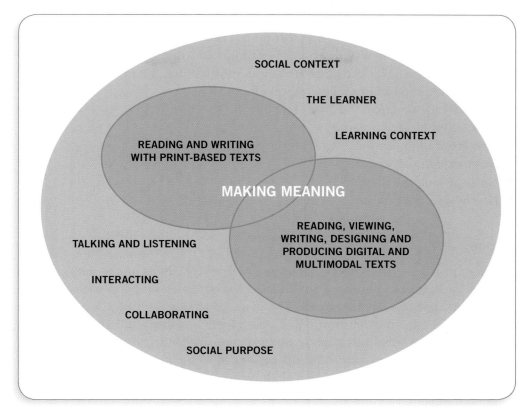

Figure 3. Multimodal literacy in classroom contexts

CLASSROOM IMPLICATIONS

The analysis of data from the research on which this book is based, further confirms this conceptualisation of multimodal literacy and demonstrates that literacy needs to be redefined within current curriculum contexts, particularly in light of the emergence of a national curriculum. Our research has enabled a more detailed description of contemporary literacy practices. As we analysed the data using the language and literacy elements of talking, listening, reading, viewing and writing, it became clear that these elements embody further dimensions when combined with digital communication technology.

Thus a comprehensive description of literacy within new communication environments has evolved from this research. The term 'multimodal literacy' indicates the way processes of language and literacy – reading, writing, talking, listening and viewing – are occurring within and around new communication media (Kress & Jewitt, 2003). Our research (Walsh 2008; 2009) has enabled a definition of multimodal literacy to be proposed with evidence from classroom data to support this definition.

These findings offered insight into new ways to describe and program for literacy learning in the twenty-first century. The chapters that follow report and analyse these findings and provide examples of the way pedagogy can be redesigned within a framework of literacy as 'multimodal'. There will be examples and discussion around the following themes:

- New literacy practices
- New texts
- Literature in multimodal contexts
- New texts in new spaces
- New classroom dynamics
- New ways of teaching.

SUMMARY

Literacy practices of students outside school reveal engagement with mobile, gaming and digital technologies with less interest in reading and writing print-based texts, particularly literature. There are educational implications for these changes in digital communication. This chapter has discussed the differences and similarities in reading print-based texts compared with multimodal texts and has shown that, while multiple modes may need to be processed for reading and writing screen-based texts, meaning-making is still the main purpose. Multimodal literacy is one way of describing reading and writing in new communcation environments. The next chapters will provide specific examples of multimodal literacy in classroom contexts.

CHAPTER 2
New literacy practices

INTRODUCTION

New literacy practices are continuing to evolve in classrooms as teachers plan ways of incorporating print with digital-based texts. These practices may include students:

- reading on screen as well as reading books
- navigating different pathways on the internet and hyperlinking to other sites
- composing and writing on screen
- transferring written text, photography or film to create a media product that is designed and edited to include text with image, sound or movement.

In such instances students are required to combine more than one skill, Within these practices, as discussed in Chapter 1, we cannot describe 'reading', 'writing' or 'viewing' as separate activities. The visual processes of reading and viewing often merge as students navigate written text, images and graphics on a screen. This integration of more than one skill is developing different literacy practices from the past where the focus was on a reading task or a writing activity. These new literacy practices require a different approach to programming and assessment. Moreover they can often involve both interactive and participatory dimensions: interactivity between modes as well as between students; and participatory in the ways students communicate and collaborate to respond to and create new texts.

This chapter provides classroom examples of new literacy practices that have been identified within our research. A particular feature of these examples is that they evolved through the way teachers planned literacy processes as part of investigations in Key Learning Areas (KLAs) within teaching/learning cycles that incorporated multimodal and digital texts.

INCORPORATING DIGITAL TEXTS
INTO THE TEACHING/LEARNING CYCLE

Programming within an integrated teaching/learning cycle is not new. What was new, within the research, was the way the teachers planned to incorporate aspects of digital technology to enable students to investigate, communicate, reflect on and produce results of their learning. The facilities of technology motivated and engaged students with visual moving screens and speedy access so that students were able to access information about 'real' events and places through virtual searches and experiences, as well as through traditional texts. Thus the building of 'field knowledge', that often occurs through concrete activities and experiences, was supported by access to virtual sites.

Investigations were prominent where English and literacy programs were linked to curriculum areas such as Science and Technology (S&T) or Human Society in Its Environment (HSIE), and Studies of Society and the Environment (SOSE). As students researched and investigated aspects of a curriculum topic, they recorded findings in written and/or digital form, and gradually worked towards creating a final media product that displayed their learning. Within this investigative process, reading and writing strategies were taught at specific stages along with appropriate oral and written language structures.

To demonstrate the changed and new literacy practices that occurred, four classroom vignettes are presented and analysed through this chapter.

VIGNETTE 1: EXPLORING ANTARCTICA

Antarctica was the focus of a program planned for Year 6 students. This was a rich investigation that required students to research for information about the geography and environment of Antarctica and the future impact of changes in the global environment. Teachers arranged for students to communicate with two scientists. One of the scientists who had been to Antarctica came to the school and spoke to the students about his experiences; while the students communicated with the other explorer in Antarctica in real time through use of *Skype* and a webcam.

Many of the students' activities through the program are described in Table 2. The left-hand column describes learning processes in the students' study of Antarctica. The right-hand column provides specific details of literacy practices, highlighting in bold font the incorporation of new literacy practices that were occurring with digital technology.

The details in Table 2 show that students were engaged in a range of different

TABLE 2. YEAR 6 HSIE/SOSE STUDY OF ANTARCTICA	
LEARNING PROCESSES	**INCORPORATION OF NEW LITERACY PRACTICES**
In their research on Antarctica, students read information books about Antarctica, researched different websites for information, with access to an Interactive White Board (IWB) as well as desktop computers, and made written notes of their learning.	Students were reading for, searching, locating and recording information in **both print and screen-based texts**. Key words and knowledge of technical vocabulary were needed with interpretation of maps and geographical areas. For information in books students need to use index, chapter headings, understand new information and interpret maps. For **screen-based reading** they needed **to scroll and select** from menu bars, **hyperlink** between screens and sites, **navigate** through maps and virtual representations of parts of Antarctica. **Hand movements** were used in **scrolling, clicking a mouse or moving items on the IWB**.
Through images, maps and videos on the IWB students were able to view parts of Antarctica, understand its geographical and environmental features and the purpose of scientific exploration.	Students were processing information from their notes to develop an **interactive map, on screen**, of a specific part of Antarctica. Students needed to understand the precise geographic aspects and the significance of the area and to **design access for others with key terms hyperlinked to sites** with further information.
In pairs, students were required to represent their information through mind maps as well as interactive maps on screen of a specific part of Antarctica.	**Writing was occurring on screen** and an **'on screen' interactive map was a different visual text** that needed to be planned and designed
Students were required to write both information reports and discussions about issues related to Antarctica and the environment.	Student **learning was interactive** and collaborative as they combined their ideas to produce information for others to access on screen.
Students' study of Antarctica was enhanced by 'real world' experiences. A professional scientist, who had explored Antarctica, visited the school and talked to the students. Students were able to communicate with another scientist at a base camp in Antarctica in real time through the facilities of a web cam and the internet. Thus specific technical vocabulary and concepts gained more relevance through the authentic experiences.	Understanding of the topic was enhanced by **virtual communication through webcam and internet. Video recording documented** students' comments on their learning.

Figure 4. Students constructing mind maps and interactive maps on screen

literacy practices. Their research was enhanced by both the 'real world' and virtual communication with scientists. Visual representations of Antarctica on the web were combined with reading and research strategies that were developed in conjunction with digital technology. Thus students were able to participate in this virtual world and to produce their own representations or 'new texts'. In this case the new texts were interactive mind maps on the screen. Figure 4 shows two stages of the development of these texts. The two top images show a student working on a mind map on an IWB of the geographic features of a specific part of Antarctica. The two lower images show students with mind maps on the computer screen that are then transferred onto the geographical areas of Antarctica as interactive maps for other students to access and learn from.

This type of investigation and production of information for other students was a cognitively demanding activity and required students to share their learning and to work together collaboratively. Teachers commented that this collaborative approach motivated students and enabled those who often were not as good at traditional reading and writing tasks to use other modes of learning. For example, one student who had learning difficulties was quick and competent at showing other students how to use the facilities of the IWB.

WHAT IS DIFFERENT ABOUT THESE NEW LITERACY PRACTICES?

Without the use of digital technology, effective learning could occur as it always has. Students could research the topic of Antarctica with information books, then record and report on their learning orally and in writing. Guest scientists could have been invited to speak to the students.

However the way digital technology was incorporated in this program enabled students to deepen their learning through authentic research that was enhanced by both the technology and the teachers' creative planning.

The processes of reading and writing for these students can be described as new literacy practices in the way that activities with print and digital texts converged. Reading on screen, particularly the viewing and manipulation of interactive maps, augmented reading for information. Recording of new information was written down and then this learning was transferred into the digital form of interactive maps for others to use. Students were not only documenting their own their learning but designing ways for others to access information and learn. While these interactive maps were an extension of semantic mapping, a reading comprehension strategy that has been well known for many years, the process of producing these within a digital geographic map required detailed, metacognitive strategies. Thus the affordances of digital technology, combined with the way teachers planned these tasks for students, enabled students to be engaged in authentic learning and literacy.

A common aspect of this example, and other examples presented in this book, was the participatory nature of student learning. The nature of many of the tasks required collaboration. This profile of collaboration was undoubtedly linked to the nature of digital communication that both invites and requires collaborative participation. Students were highly motivated to work together, not only to use the technology, but also to create products that were evidence of their learning in the particular curriculum area.

· ·

REFLECTION

Within integrated approaches that incorporate real-world experiences and digital technologies students can be highly motivated. Often this work occurs in groups. How do teachers ensure that:

- essential aspects of reading and writing strategies are taught explicitly?
- individual students are assessed effectively?
- teaching and assessing new literacy practices do not conflict with essential skills and strategies required for student progress within national curriculum guidelines?

· ·

Antarctica is representative of many programs that occurred during the research. There were a range of investigations that demonstrated these new literacy

VIGNETTE 2: VISIT ASIA

In this example Year 6 students were required to investigate different Asian countries. The teachers facilitated the investigations so that students were required to develop their own questions and interests about specific countries that they were to research and these were linked to geographical, social and cultural issues. Students were able to enhance their research through the virtual images on *Google Earth* accessed on the IWB along with web and book searches for information about the Asian country they had chosen. Online interviews, using the webcam, were arranged with adults, known to the teachers, who had travelled in Asia. These interviews augmented the authenticity of their investigation. The program culminated with an 'Asian Travel Expo' with parents, other teachers and students invited to view the outcomes of the students' investigations. The Expo motivated students to perfect their final presentations on their learning which incorporated reading, research, writing, design, photography and filming. Final products included written and visual displays, PowerPoint presentations, digital narratives with animations, podcasts, vodcasts, and videos.

practices. Vignette 2 shows how Stage 3 students developed research on Asian countries and then produced an 'Asian Travel Expo'.

During this investigation, aspects of reading and writing were occurring within students' search for information about the country they were researching. However, new literacy practices were occurring in that reading and writing were combined with varieties of digital media. Reading was occurring with paper-based texts and on screen with an IWB, webcam, web searches and viewing of video clips. Similarly writing was occurring on paper and on screen combined with visual media. To illustrate the way content, skills and media were combined for students' learning, it is useful to consider some examples from the teachers' program. These examples are taken from the teachers' PowerPoint summary of the outcomes of their program on 'Visit Asia'. Figure 5 shows the range of topics that student were to investigate in each country while Figure 6 shows activities and resources students could use to present their findings.

Figures 5 and 6 demonstrate a comprehensive range of topics as well as media used while Figures 7 and 8 present some glimpses of the students 'journey' in their investigations and the final travel Expo. Figure 7 displays examples of the students researching, designing and making items that represented a feature of the particular country, or producing texts to record their learning.

Figure 8 presents some images from the Asia Expo showing a range of ways

Topics To Cover

Food	Location	Traditional Clothing	Climate
Landmarks	Celebrations & Culture	Religion	Language
Flora	Relationship with Australia	Fauna	Flag
Currency	National Anthem	Population	Government

Politics	The Environment	History	Education
Famous People	Sport	Economic Climate	Imports & Exports

Figure 5. Topics to be researched for the Asian country chosen

Equipment Available

Interviews	Podcasts & Vodcasts	Drama	Puppetry
Powerpoint	Blogs	Painting	Sculpture
Animation	Photo Board	Dance	Poster
Brochures	Graphs	Diagrams	Song
Music	Storytelling	Advertisements – written, visual or recorded.	Models

Figure 6. Print and media resources available for students

in which students displayed features of different countries. In the case of the Asia Expo the final display tables were designed with visual features of particular countries and included information about the country with charts, costumes, models, written information, digital narratives with animation and videos.

This learning process is typical of many of the programs in that students were engaged in reading and researching a topic in a KLA area and were required to write and report on their learning by producing a text that could consist of print or a variety of media.

Figure 7. Students engaged in their research

Figure 8. Photos of some exhibits on the "Expo" day

The two teachers who planned the Visit Asia program were pleased and surprised at the changes that had occurred in the classroom literacy practices.

COMMENT
We learnt that the students were open to new ways of learning. The students were extended and they surprised themselves as well as us with the amount of knowledge they gained. We were surprised by just how much their writing and communication skills improved during the term.

READING IN A DIGITAL ENVIRONMENT: VIEWING, SEARCHING AND RESPONDING

In the digital environment reading takes on a different process. As shown in the examples of Antarctica and Visit Asia, the process of reading on screen was clearly different from reading print-based texts, as has been shown in other studies (Kress, 2003; Walsh, 2006; Bearne et al, 2007). Processes such as viewing, searching, browsing, scrolling, clicking and responding to multiple pathways from hyperlinks is very different from the linear processing of words on a page. These classroom examples confirm that reading on screen entails an intricacy in the way meaning is more often embedded within a combination of visual, graphic and textual modes.

In their investigations students were engaged in reading both print-based and screen-based texts, however these reading activities were usually linked to other talking, listening or writing activities in some way. While a reader's interaction with a text has long been established as an important aspect of comprehension, interaction was occurring in further ways. Reading and viewing offered a more participatory role in the way teachers programmed. Tasks were such that students were required to interact with either the print or digital texts that they were accessing, as well as to interact with each other. Students' responses usually occurred either in group situations or in online discussions. These examples show that reading in a digital environment is a multifaceted process.

EARLY LITERACY LEARNERS IN A DIGITAL ENVIRONMENT: 'DIGI-VEGIES' AND 'DIGI-CHICKS'

Two teachers in the one school worked with their Kindergarten and Year One class, respectively, to have their students learn and develop literacy through investigation. The Kindergarten students were able to develop their beginning reading skills within the context of hands-on learning experiences as they learnt about planting a vegetable garden within the theme of 'digi-vegies'. The Year 1 students investigated the life cycle of chickens. Each of these examples is now discussed. Vignette 3 summarises the teacher's program that occurred over several weeks. As the young Kindergarten students experienced and observed the planting of seedlings there was a merging of print and digital reading practices.

VIGNETTE 3: 'DIGI-VEGIES'

As students helped the teacher to plant seedlings they listened to instructions; watched demonstrations; photographed and talked about the planting process; observed and described seeds with use of digital microscopes and digi cams; and saved photographs on computer files. Students looked at examples of seeds, plants and vegetables in information books; discussed planting procedures using picture cards and digital photographs; and saved digital recordings with the webcam of students talking about the procedure of planting. The teacher modelled reading of related literature with continual attention to word recognition, phonics and sight vocabulary. Students' journalled with the teacher their observations on the planting of seedlings assisted by records from the digi cams and wrote short descriptions. These written descriptions were illustrated with drawings or pictures saved on screen from the digital microscope or digi cams. Students progressed from writing simple sentences to the joint writing of stages of a procedure.

This rich learning environment meant that these early learners engaged in reading through a great deal of talking, listening, observing and viewing with concrete materials, print and digital texts. There was a constant interchange between sensory experiences, written and screen modes of images and words. Students were learning about the planting and growth of seedlings. At the same time they were introduced to words, letters and their sounds, simple clauses and sentences that the teacher modelled to accompany their observations and photographs. These reading activities occurred with introduction to pictures, diagrams, written explanations and stories in books. These reading and learning experiences were linked to models of writing with class joint construction and writing by individual students who wrote sentences of aspects of procedures accompanied by photos or drawings. Figure 9 shows two students making clay figures of vegetables at different stages of growth and talking about the way to do this. Figure 10 shows a student presenting his learning about how vegetables grow on to the computer screen.

Figure 9. Students representing the growth of vegetables with clay

The photo in Figure 10 demonstrates a typical example of multimodal literacy. The student is shown producing a text on screen while using a visual, print-based record of his observations of the different features of seedlings.

Figure 10. Transferring from paper to screen

This coherence of literacy and learning experiences was evident in the Year 1 students' observations of chickens growing over several weeks. Vignette 4 summarises the investigations of these students who were led to conduct investigations through real life experience, books and technology.

VIGNETTE 4: 'DIGI-CHICKS'

Students observed the life cycle of chickens from the embryo in an egg to full growth and listened to explanations of different stages learning new vocabulary. Observations were enhanced by use of light table, magnifying glass and a digital microscope with images transferred onto computer screen and saved. These photos with other photos from the webcam were saved and used for an online diary in *Voice Thread* (voicethread.com). Teachers extended oral language structures of sequencing and explaining and scaffolded these with audio recorded explanations on teacher-made postcards. Students read and viewed information books, class displays of posters, display of pop-up cards, and information in the online journals. The teacher modelled reading of a range of texts, reading and viewing internet sites and video. Print and digital displays were used as scaffolds for joint writing of explanations and for claymation.

This example demonstrates the richness of learning that occurred when literacy activities, modes and texts were connected in a meaningful way. The photograph in Figure 11 shows the clay figures of chickens. Students were making the figures to represent different stages of a chicken's growth, using segments from the written text of the class joint construction as a guide. The students had to read the print out of the written text and match it with the clay figure they were to make.

The clay figures were then used for the class claymation about the life cycle of a chicken. Claymation is a popular media form with students and it involves animation using clay figures. Objects or characters are moulded from clay or similar products such as plasticine and are supported by wire structures underneath. In a detailed process, known as 'stop motion animation', a series of still pictures of the photographed clay objects being replayed very quickly creates the illusion of movement. Claymation was used in several classes during this research and further examples are detailed in Chapter 3.

Such integration of learning activities is not new in education, however the combination of all the activities that were transferred into digital texts provided the opportunity for a cohesive interrelationship between learning experiences.

Figure 11. Clay figures made to represent the written descriptions

This showed that a holistic approach to learning can be very important for young learners. The teachers' comment on these two programs reveal the significance of their detailed, creative planning:

COMMENT
Students in Kindergarten and Year One were well able to transfer their skills to unfamiliar technologies and applications. They were confident in recognising their own skills, taking risks, experimenting with the unknown and sharing learnings.

It is evident that in this program, as with others mentioned through the chapter, students were engaged in various aspects of literacy – reading and writing – along with other practices enabled and enhanced by digital communications technology. Writing on screen incorporated images and graphics so that students needed to consider layout and design, as well as the most appropriate choice of each to suit their audience. Reading and viewing were combined with searching and responding. With the collaborative approach to investigating and reporting on their learning, talking and listening were important for ensuring learning about content as well as effective communication with their teacher and peers with both spoken and written forms of language. Thus traditional aspects of literacy were being expanded to include other modes and processes.

THE NATURE OF NEW LITERACY PRACTICES

The four vignettes of teaching programs examined in this chapter, *Antarctica*, *Visit Asia*, *Digi-vegies* and *Digi-chicks* allowed for new practices of literacy to be integral to students' investigations. Figure 12 represents the integral nature of student research with use of digital and print media. The inner section depicts the process of investigation and research while the outer section indicates those aspects of reading, viewing, searching, hyperlinking, writing and recording with both print and digital media that were blended within the research.

As the diagram shows reading, viewing, understanding, recording and interacting were often a simultaneous, interchangeable processes within investigations when combined with the affordances of digital texts. As the teachers' programs were planned and implemented there was a holistic process through the stages of students investigating, then recording, reporting and producing results of their learning. Language and literacy learning were embedded within a progressive, continuous learning environment over several weeks. Figure 13 represents the process, highlighting both the literacy strategies needed along with the use of digital technology at different stages.

The continuous, interconnected nature of the language and literacy learning processes, represented in Figure 13 was not sequential but recursive at different stages through many of the teaching programs. In each of these programs students were incorporating digital technology to research, read, write and produce results of their learning. These are indeed examples of multimodal learning environments where students' work is blended with real life experiences and web enhanced. This holistic process was evident in the teachers' programs

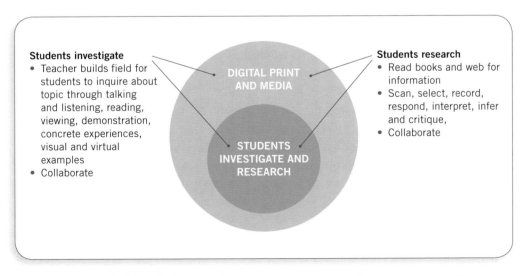

Figure 12. The integral relationship between investigations through print and digital media

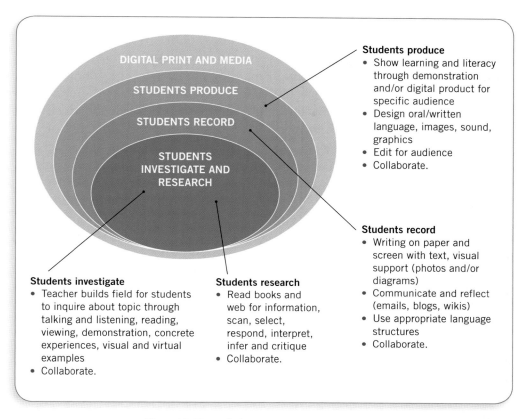

Students produce
- Show learning and literacy through demonstration and/or digital product for specific audience
- Design oral/written language, images, sound, graphics
- Edit for audience
- Collaborate.

Students record
- Writing on paper and screen with text, visual support (photos and/or diagrams)
- Communicate and reflect (emails, blogs, wikis)
- Use appropriate language structures
- Collaborate.

Students investigate
- Teacher builds field for students to inquire about topic through talking and listening, reading, viewing, demonstration, concrete experiences, visual and virtual examples
- Collaborate.

Students research
- Read books and web for information, scan, select, respond, interpret, infer and critique
- Collaborate.

Figure 13. The holistic nature of multimodal literacy

while assessment became a more continuous process as evidence of students' development over time was recorded.

A common aspect of this example, and other examples presented in this book, was the participatory nature of student learning. The nature of many of the tasks required collaboration. This profile of collaboration was undoubtedly linked to the nature of digital communication that both invites and requires collaborative participation. Students were highly motivated to work together, not only to use the technology, but also to create products that were evidence of their learning in the particular curriculum area.

The role of the Interactive White Boards (IWB) for new literacy practices

During 2009, Interactive White Boards (IWBs) were more available in many of the classes than in previous years and the accessibility provided by this new technology allowed many of the teachers and students to be more creative. For example, *Google Earth* was able to assist students' conceptualisation of time and space in some programs. In several programs the use of the IWB was an important resource for whole class learning and discussions as well as for group searches. An IWB, with its large and interactive screen, allows for instant information to be searched for, read and viewed by a whole class or a group of students. Comparisons can be made between different sites; and between information obtained and students' own experiments. Information can be selected and arranged on the screen and saved, thus creating a new compilation of information text on screen. Reading for information was facilitated by the visual and graphic features of the IWB, where a group of students could display, consider and discuss the information. Students can respond, understand and interact with the visual, kinaesthetic and auditory modes in virtual space and time. This is a clear example of the multimodal nature of new literacy practices. The IWB offers a range of uses such as speedy access, display and use of stored software and files as well as the projection of sites from the internet. Files from digital cameras, VCRs, DVDs and CD-ROMS can be easily transferred and displayed. Its multimodal features and interactivity through the touch screen is speedy and dynamic allowing for the exploration and transformation of files into other multimedia products.

SUMMARY

The examples presented in this chapter reveal the potential of developing holistic learning and literacy process for students of different ages. These examples show that:

- students were engaged in reading print and screen-based texts and this reading involved the skills of researching and reading for information
- students needed to skim and scan for information with books but to scroll and navigate websites as well as be able to select the relevance of particular websites.
- reading on screen included scrolling, selecting from the menu bar or icons, hyperlinking between sites, navigating, and using the mouse or touch feature of an IWB
- written records were on paper as well as on screen and digital facilities were used for final products of students' learning.

These processes can be described as students constructing 'new literacy practices' that are clearly multimodal. What was new and different, was not the technology itself, but the way students' learning was articulated through both traditional and new media. 'New texts' were being created and these 'new texts', detailed further in Chapter 3 evolved from progressive investigations that were planned to engage students' curiosity and interest.

CHAPTER 3
New texts

INTRODUCTION

Film and video have been an important part of education for some time. Now, with easier and cheaper access to new technologies, digital products can be used quite differently to create new types of texts. The facilities of digital photography and video, particularly *Flip* cameras and IWBs with associated software on laptops, allow for editing and manipulation in a variety of multimedia. Students are able to edit and incorporate music and sound effects with available software such as *MovieMaker*, *Audacity*, *2Create*, *2Publish*, *Garage Band* or *Comic Life*.

In our research project several new texts were used and produced – new in terms of being different from the texts school students have written or produced in the past and new in that they were the first time many teachers and students had created them. In this chapter there are examples of how easily accessible software such as *2Publish* enabled young students to design posters as persuasive 'text types', while other students produced digital narratives or developed explanations through claymation. New texts were created and these allowed students to not just record but to construct, represent and reflect on their learning. Several examples such as podcasts, digital texts, posters and pamphlets, video texts, digital narratives and claymation, many of which were developed within studies of literature, are described and analysed in this chapter.

PODCASTS

Podcasting has become a popular development within Web 2.0 technology (Kervin, 2009) and enables the use of a range of modes in the production of a multimedia experience. Vignette 5 demonstrates how a teacher and students worked through podcasting to incorporate different modes of print and digital

VIGNETTE 5: YEAR 3 PODASTS

In pairs, the students were required to plan, draft, develop, refine, produce and review an eight-minute podcast suitable for sharing with a broad audience. The final podcasts were uploaded to *iTunes* as well as onto the school's intranet. Each podcast had to consist of an introduction, an information report about an Australian spider, a serialised section of a narrative and a conclusion that could include jokes or puzzles. Each segment of the podcast had to be researched and written with the teacher at first modelling and scaffolding the different text types. The segments were then designed into storyboards, incorporating written text with visuals such as photographs or drawings, before recording could commence. Audio recording was edited along with sound effects and music.

texts within literacy and curriculum learning. In this example Year 3 students were engaged in a range of literacy tasks of researching, planning and writing texts for broadcasting while learning about the technology of using audio and video files to produce their podcasts.

There were a range of literacy practices needed for the development and final production of each podcast and these are highlighted in Figure 14 which details the range of language and literacy practices needed for this task.

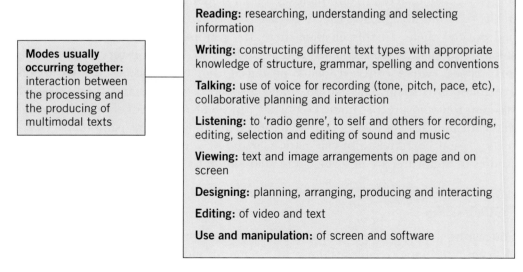

Modes usually occurring together: interaction between the processing and the producing of multimodal texts

Reading: researching, understanding and selecting information

Writing: constructing different text types with appropriate knowledge of structure, grammar, spelling and conventions

Talking: use of voice for recording (tone, pitch, pace, etc), collaborative planning and interaction

Listening: to 'radio genre', to self and others for recording, editing, selection and editing of sound and music

Viewing: text and image arrangements on page and on screen

Designing: planning, arranging, producing and interacting

Editing: of video and text

Use and manipulation: of screen and software

Figure 14. Range of language and literacy practices in the development of a podcast

In Figure 14 which details the literacy practices needed for the development of a podcast (Walsh, 2008), the right-hand column highlights all the processes students were engaged in throughout the podcasting task. Those aspects that are commonly referred to as components of an English curriculum – reading, writing, viewing, talking and listening – occurred along with aspects of designing, manipulating and using software on laptops. This example demonstrates a difference from previous classroom literacy practices with print-based texts and this difference cannot be attributed just to the additional use of technology.

> **The principle difference about this new text, the podcast, lies in the way traditional aspects of literacy were combined with other modalities and semiotic systems. These processes involve a convergence – an interconnection and interdependence between the modalities of written text, image and sound.**

In the podcast the mode of sound was predominant as students incorporated written text and visuals into the audio production. Students needed to learn the use of voice with aspects of tone, intonation, pause, pitch, modulation and stress and combine these with simultaneous integration of music and sound effects. There was the further visual process of all this occurring on screen as the music and sound effects needed to be edited and synchronised through the use of the *GarageBand* software, the visuals loaded through *Comic Life* software, and the eventual uploading of this product onto a website.

At the same time the use of written text was integral as a dominant mode since the students had to write different text types within the overall podcast text and plan the sequencing of the language for their audio production. If we consider the way writing, an essential aspect of literacy, was developed during the podcasting it is evident that the requirements for writing have changed within new modes of communication. Figure 15 illustrates the complexities involved in the writing processes that occurred for the students who were writing for an audio broadcast. The bold typeface indicates where aspects of digital technology occurred within the processes of reading and writing.

A classroom writing task need no longer be seen as writing a particular genre or text type to be edited and produced on paper. The podcasting process itself introduced a new genre that incorporated other genres. At the same time traditional or 'basic' conventions of writing, particularly text structure, sentences, grammar, spelling and punctuation were maintained. The students worked through a progressive process of learning with the teacher modelling and scaffolding structures and conventions at different stages.

This whole process demonstrates the multimodality of literacy, where modes

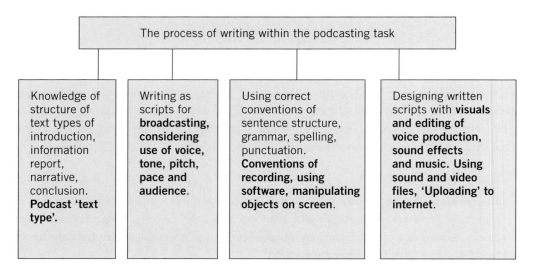

Figure 15. Writing and producing within new modes of communication (Walsh, 2008, P.105)

converge. It was evident that these eight-year-old students achieved a depth of literacy and learning about information reports and narratives along with other skills in the design and production of the podcasting process. Engagement of students was high, particularly for many boys whom the teacher had found were often disengaged from classroom learning. There was cohesion in the literacy and learning that occurred. This was indeed an example of multimodal literacy that involved students working together: talking, listening, planning, reading, researching, designing, writing and producing using both print and digital modes.

· ·

REFLECTION: THE MULTIMODALITY OF NEW TEXTS

This one example, typical of other teachers' programs in the research shows the convergence and interconnection between modes of reading, writing, talking listening, viewing while using both print and digital texts. Digital technology offers the facilities for literacy to be more multimodal than previously, providing opportunities for response to and manipulation of the visual, graphic, sound and kinaesthetic modes.

· ·

As demonstrated in Chapter 2, these new texts allowed for literacy to occur within a holistic process where talking, listening, reading and writing were interrelated, At the same time explicit teaching of skills and strategies could be taught at the point of need to the whole class, groups or individual students.

WRITTEN TEXTS MERGING INTO DIGITAL TEXTS

The detailed discussion of the podcasting example reveals the emergence of a new text type. Other examples of new types of texts are shown in the discussion of Vignettes 6 and 7. Here teachers of younger and older grades developed students' understanding of the structures of explanation, persuasion, procedure and description through written, visual, dramatic and digital forms.

Figure 16 demonstrates the way students recorded their learning about water and recycling by designing cycle wheels through the use of digital software to visually represent their learning.

These representations in Figure 16 were developed on screen and could be printed as a resource for students. These examples demonstrate how students could express their knowledge through different modes of graphics, colour, images and words while developing their understanding of the Science content as well as the structure and language of explanations. Along with this visual organisation of their learning, students were required to write explanations of the processes they had investigated. The students went through different stages of writing explanation texts and Figure 17 shows an example of one student's written explanation with a visual diagram to support the explanation.

This example, where the student has used a diagram to support the written explanation, is a multimodal text produced by the student on paper. Both verbal and visual texts show the student's understanding of the sequential process of the water cycle.

VIGNETTE 6: CONSERVING AND RECYCLING WATER

A variety of written and digital texts were created in a Year 2 class where students studied different aspects of conserving the environment, particularly looking at conserving water and recycling. In investigating ways of conserving the environment, these seven-year-old students discussed their new learning about the impact of changes in the environment and selected initiatives that would help persuade others to be more vigilant in protecting the environment. The teacher built the students' understanding gradually through showing them how to research information from books, the media and the internet. Students learnt the meaning of new concepts and used technical language related to learning about aspects such as recycling and waste reduction. Problem solving occurred within students' investigations and as they negotiated ways of communicating the importance of recycling. Drama was used and filmed to demonstrate the need for conservation and students produced explanation and persuasive texts on paper, screen and video.

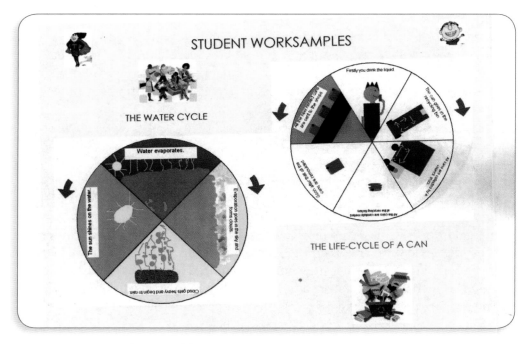

Figure 16. Digital representations to explain cyclic processes

One of the outcomes of the students' investigations was the production of creative posters, using *2Publish* software, to persuade others to recycle. So students moved from extending their learning through explanations to more critical thinking by considering the impact of waste on the environment. Some examples of their persuasive posters are shown in Figure 18.

Even at this young age it is evident that the students understood the importance of arranging text and images to persuade and explain. Each poster consists of the same visual layout of a heading, two images and explanatory text. However there is variation in the imaginative use of either images or words. For example the caption 'Be cool don't be a fool' shows creative enthusiasm through words while in the third poster two contrasting images are used to demonstrate the correct and incorrect procedures for recycling. Students' creativity was further extended as they produced a video on an environmental 'Superhero' with careful planning and rehearsal of dialogue, costumes and setting preceding the filming and editing.

The teacher's photographs of students planning and designing is shown in Figure 19. Students were required to produce a digital narrative related to conserving the environment.

To be able to complete this task students needed to understand the importance of conserving the environment, the structure and language needed for their

Name: Anne   Date: 28/5/08

The water cycle

The water cycle is a movement
of water. Water is a type of liquid.
First the clouds rains. Then rain fills up
the lakes, sea, ocean and land. Next the sun
shies and evapororates some water.
After that it forms a cloud.
                              rains. The cycle
As a result it ʌ are it never stops.
Water is important because if we
didn't have water we would die.

Figure 17. The written explanation of the water cycle

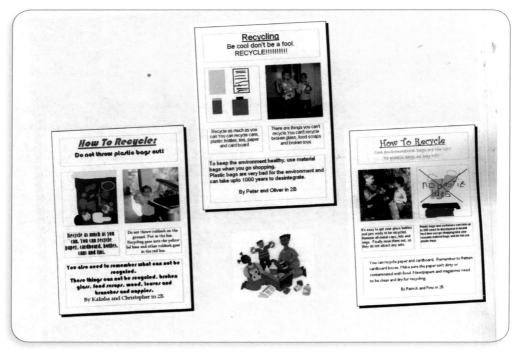

Figure 18. Posters designed for recycling

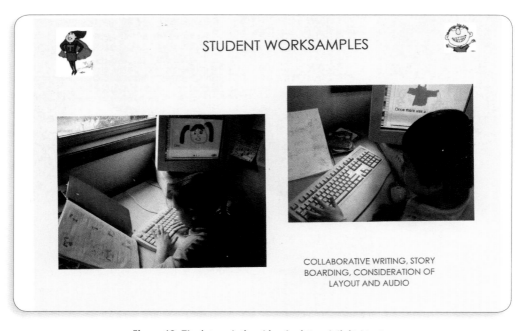

Figure 19. The interrelationship of print and digital texts.

narrative and the components of a digital narrative. The combination of writing, planning layout, developing the visual sequence of a storyboard with audio requires an understanding of design and selection to suit the purpose of the final text.

Further examples of new texts are described through the discussion of Vignette 7.

VIGNETTE 7: PICASSO AND CUBISM

Different types of digital texts were designed and produced by students in two Year 5 and 6 classes that were combined for a study of Picasso and Cubism within an integrated unit for English and Creative Arts. Teachers guided and scaffolded students' research on the life of Picasso and an understanding of Cubism. The students were able to choose different ways to demonstrate their learning through written work and digital products, which could be accessed digitally or online. Students' responses demonstrated a range of print and digital literacy practices as they:

- examined text-image arrangements in print and digital texts
- evaluated individual art works of Picasso
- understood the structure and language of the particular text types of procedure and literary description
- were introduced to blogging developed an understanding of the importance of layout, colour and arrangement of visual and digital texts

---

Some examples of work by different groups are displayed in Figures 20, 21, 22 and 23.

Figure 20 shows examples of pamphlets that students created on the life of Picasso.

Using the software program *2Publish* students needed to combine layout, headings and illustrations with appropriate writing style and structure to succinctly convey the important features of Picasso's art to readers. To be able to produce this work, students needed to have a thorough understanding of Picasso's work, to organise their writing within the layout and format of a brochure, and to write and arrange text and images to engage the interests of the readers.

Another group of students wrote and produced a procedural text on 'How to create a cubist artwork'. Students combined their knowledge of the language and grammatical structures of written procedures with visual and graphic design. Figures 19 and 20 are extracts from this digital procedural text, 'Producing a Picasso'.

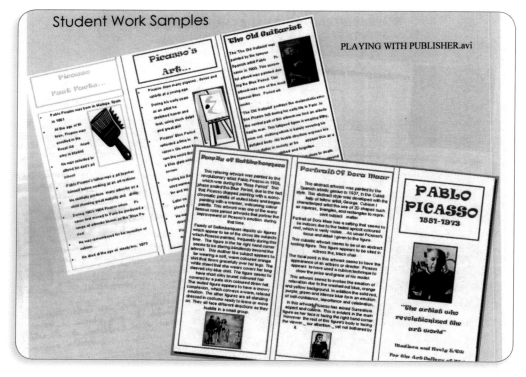

Figure 20

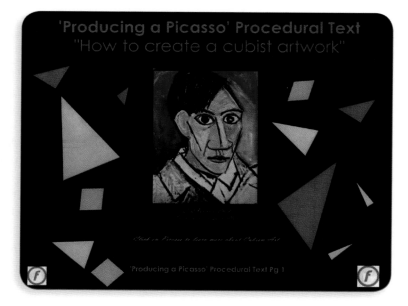

Figure 21

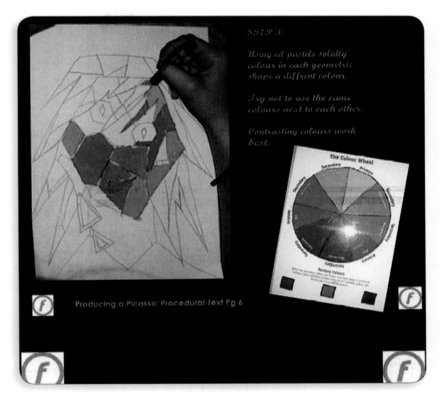

Figure 22

Figures 21 and 22 are extracts from a detailed digital instructional text for other students to use. An understanding of cubism was needed to be able to communicate this procedure. This whole text is cleverly designed using a cubist style of colour, angles and shapes. The title screen, Figure 21, is appropriate to the Picasso portrait used. The use of hypertext links demonstrates the students' awareness of the structure of a digital text. In Figure 22 'step 3' shows the specific planning with storyboard, photographs and words needed for a reader to understand the procedures to create their own cubist art work. This is an example of students producing work for a real audience.

A complex work was developed by another group of students who produced a video relating to one of Picasso's major paintings, the 'Family of Saltimbanques' (Figure 23). This video was a gradual construction as students role-played and photographed depictions of themselves as the circus figures in Picasso's painting. These photographs were then transferred into a photo story and, through Movie Maker, used to create a video on an IWB.

The final text, a video played on an IWB, was a product that incorporated different layers of texts with photographs and audio commentary and sound

Figure 23

effects merging into the final product. Imaginative ideas are particularly evident in the photographs that are meant to represent this period of Picasso's work. All these examples support comments from their teachers.

COMMENT
Students were immersed in their learning - reading, viewing, interpreting and producing paper, electronic and live texts.

Both these examples of Vignettes 6 and 7 occurred in the one school so that teachers in different classes worked in a team as part of the research. Thus they shared ideas and applied them to suit the age levels of their students as they considered how to engage students in effective literacy practices while having students produce new types of texts with digital technology. Here is a combined statement from the three teachers about the impact of working together:

COMMENT

We explored a range of learning structures, which engaged and immersed students in rich learning experiences within a contemporary classroom. Through the integration of various technology and digital media we were able to foster a learning environment, which promoted individual creativity, risk taking, collaboration, negotiation and problem solving.

VIDEOS CREATED AS NEW TEXTS TO CONSTRUCT LEARNING

Video was used within several programs to film investigations, to provide recounts, explanations or procedures, and for students to reflect on their learning. Figure 24 shows a scene from an excursion that was incorporated into a final video that Year 4 students produced about the causes and results of British Colonisation.

In this program video was used as both a process for learning and a final product. Not only did it serve as a visual 'recount' of the students' excursion it became a visual document of the students' enactment of the historical period as, with costumes and 'identity' cards, they role-played characters from the time. The students used these digital records, from digital photographs and videos with *Flip* cameras, to write a factual recount, as a newspaper report, of the excursion to the Rocks in Sydney. The recounts were then developed into storyboard and into a digital text using *2Create a story* within the *Smart Board Notebook* or *Photostory 3* as shown in Figure 25, which is the teacher's representation of this process:

Figure 24. Enacting aspects of British Colonisation

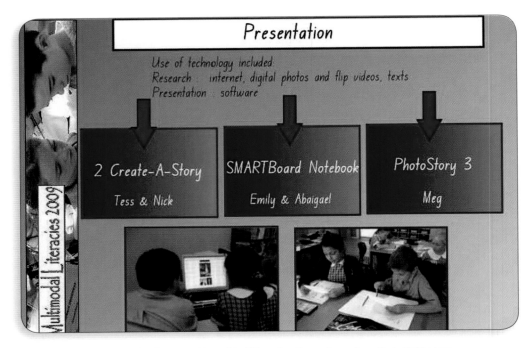

Figure 25. Students working with different software to produce their digital text

All these digital texts were then accessible to other students through the software of the IWB, in this case a *Smart Board*. Figure 26 shows a class display of students' work in the form of written, visual and digital texts.

There were several other examples where teachers used video as an integral part of learning within the program as well as for students to produce a final DVD for an audience. For example in a study of the Science topic of Light, four teachers brought their Year 4 classes together each day for five weeks to integrate literacy into students' learning with research and experiments that were about aspects of the phenomenon of light. The image in Figure 27 shows an example of students conducting an experiment while Figure 28 shows students searching for information on Light through web sites on an interactive white board (IWB). The students tagged specific still images and added text on the screen to explain the procedures for their investigations.

This process itself, of recording their learning through the research, was creating a new type of text, a digital video diary. In a further example Year 5 students, who were studying China, were required in groups to complete a spoken procedure with a demonstration. The filming of these procedures in most cases required student to demonstrate a recipe for a Chinese meal. Each group's film was collated into a class movie and a snapshot from this video is displayed in Figure 29.

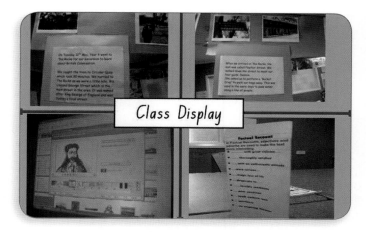

Figure 26. Written, visual and digital recounts of British Colonisation

Figure 27. Investigating features of light

Figure 28. Reading and researching with the IWB

REFLECTION: WHAT IS NEW ABOUT THIS USE OF VIDEO?

Previously students would have studied the topics and written reports or presented their learning orally, with occasional use of photography or video. With the increased accessibility of technology students were able to record their learning through video, as well as through writing, and to communicate this learning to an audience. In several cases digital photographs were inserted into Windows *MovieMaker* and produced as a video with sound, including voice-over, sound effects and music. In other cases episodes were filmed and edited with a mobile *Flip* camera or a video camera. Video segments by different groups were produced as short movies or were edited into a class DVD. These were then saved as digital texts that could be accessed easily for further learning and for assessment. While the final production of a video was not necessarily the main focus, students were highly motivated to demonstrate their work for a specific audience.

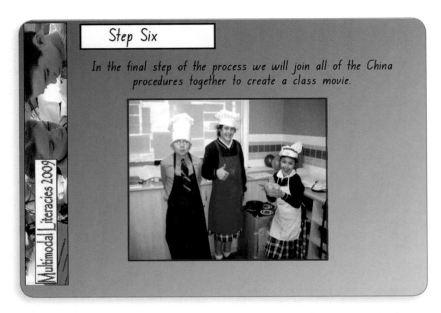

Figure 29. An example from the video students made of a 'spoken procedure'

Figure 30. Filming the effect of light and shadow

Figure 31. Writing a script together

Figure 32. Students editing video

Depending on the needs and year level of the students, there were specific aspects of literacy strategies developed within programs where teachers had students use video. Figure 30 shows students using a *Flip* camera in the playground. Although the video file from this sequence was included in a final DVD, at this stage it was an instance of students filming the effect of light to create shadows.

As students were learning about the scientific phenomenon they were learning how to use the video camera to present the information by composing the image effectively with appropriate camera angles. For this footage to be used for the final production of a DVD it had to be planned within a sequence with continuity, sound effects and voice-over to present the concept of 'light and shadows' to an audience. Thus a script needed to be written and planned, as shown in Figure 31, and this small footage would be edited, as shown in Figure 32, within the overall DVD, 'Light Fantastic', that was created by the teachers and students.

The 'new text' in this case is a DVD, the final product that has involved research, recording and producing with reading and writing at different stages on paper and on screen. Apart from understanding the scientific content the students needed to learn the effect of different types of camera shots, angles and continuity as well as the whole process of editing film for the most effective communication which, in the above example, was to explain and comment on the various functions of light.

Such a total production is itself an aspect of new literacy practices: a hybrid text or in fact a new 'text type' that incorporates other text type structures. Again, this is an example of the integral relationship between learning and technology and how literacy has changed within digital communication.

Overall, video was being used as a new text: as a specific tool for learning and as a medium of communication, augmenting oral and written reports of students' learning.

DIGITAL STORYTELLING WITH ANIMATION AND CLAYMATION

New texts were being developed through animation in several instances. For example a group of students who were studying Asia created a digital narrative of the students' version of an Indonesian folk story, as shown in Figure 33. In this image the green item on the left-hand side is a seed that grows into a fish.

As students developed digital narratives, different types of animation were used and extended students' understanding of the structure of narratives. The need to produce a narrative in a digital form with text, images and sound required

Figure 33. Student's digital narrative of an Indonesian folk tale

students to be succinct and cohesive in presenting the sequential story, the significant parts of plot and development of climactic stages, appropriate setting, features of characters and contrast. Claymation, as described in Chapter 2, was a popular form of animation. It was used in four programs in 2009 as teachers developed students' understanding of the structure of specific text types such as procedure, description, explanation or narrative. Table 3 lists examples of the way claymation was used in these programs.

TABLE 3. NEW TEXTS WITH CLAYMATION OR ANIMATION	
Kindergarten – 'On the Move'; Text type: Procedure and description	Used to describe the movement of different objects.
Year 2 – 'Unreliable narrators'; Text type: Narrative	Used to create a fairy tale narrative.
Year 4 – 'Light Fantastic'; Text type: Explanation	Used to explain the phenomenon of light.
Years 5 and 6 – 'Natural Disasters'; Text type: Explanation	Used to explain the cause and effect of different types of natural disasters.

Embedding these text types within a claymation was a process that involved reading, writing, photography, script writing, making and designing clay figures and scenes, organisation of the whole procedure, filming with voice-over and sound effects and final editing. Thus while each product incorporated structures of specific text types, claymation itself can be described as a new media text, or text type, with classroom applications for literacy and learning.

Figures 34 and 35 are examples of claymation that occurred during the research. Figure 34 shows Year 4 students developing a claymation to explain an aspect of their study of Light while Figure 35 is an image from the 'Billy Cart Race Track' story developed by two Kindergarten students. This was a result of

Figure 34. Creating a claymation to demonstrate 'Light'

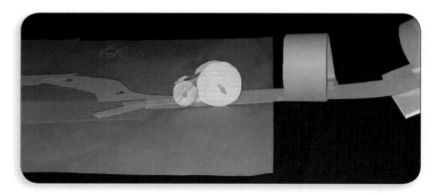

Figure 35. A photo of a clay billy cart moving along a track

the Kindergarten program 'On the Move' that is described in more detail in Chapter 6.

These claymations provided students with a medium to construct their understanding creatively through technology. As well as designing figures and scenes and organising the photographs, students had to be able to write a sequential script, in the appropriate genre, manage the editing and timing of each photograph, add voice-overs and sound effects or music, often produced within *MovieMaker*. The Kindergarten examples showed that the young students could achieve all of these tasks.

CARTOONS AND STORYBOARDS

The examples discussed in this chapter demonstrate that digital technologies allow students to transfer information from one medium to another. Cartooning and storyboarding allow this transference with programs such as *Comiclife* providing the structure for either. Some teachers used frames as structures for students to transfer narratives with illustrations into cartoons. Providing a limit of six frames, for example, ensured students had to be economical in their presentation of the main features of a story. The addition of speech bubbles for dialogue could add humour or suspense.

Even more than cartoons, storyboarding was used by teachers as an essential process for students planning to produce many of the digital texts, particularly videos and claymations. Storyboarding is a process that connects writing on paper to writing on screen, actually enabling the blending of written with visual and digital texts. Within the process of writing and preparing for a final product on screen, whether PowerPoint, blog, wiki, animation or dramatised movie – storyboarding was frequently used as a bridge between writing first drafts or ideas and the final product. In several instances of storyboarding, students made use of IWB software and the software program *Audacity* for incorporating sound effects. Figures 36 and 37 show some examples of storyboarding that were part of programs that will be referred to in the next two chapters.

Storyboarding is another skill, in fact another text type that requires students to have an organised structure with logical sequencing, continuity, development of stages, appropriate language to suit the purpose, a clear balance between written and visual text, and an understanding of design. In one instance, Year 3 students' storyboarding was confined to nine frames for their claymation film. A comment from one of the students is of interest:

COMMENT
When I get to use my hands to play with the clay, I remember the story better.

Figure 36

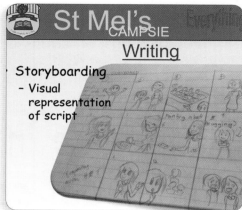

Figure 37

This comment is a telling reminder of how tactile experiences support learning. In this case reading and writing were interrelated with the concrete materials, books, the touch screen of the IWB and digital animation.

SUMMARY

The affordances of digital technologies allowed for a range of hybrid and new texts to be developed such as:

- podcasts and vodcasts
- posters and pamphlets
- cartoons, comics, videos
- digital narratives
- claymations
- storyboards.

These were developed to highlight learning in particular curriculum areas. The multimodality of these new texts meant that literacy often entailed the transference of written texts into digital form with different modes occurring together.

CHAPTER 4
Literature in multimodal contexts

INTRODUCTION

> Through literature I become a thousand people yet remain myself.
> *C.S. Lewis*

Literature has long been considered an essential aspect of the teaching of English. For the very young it presents patterns of stories and language that introduce children to representations of real-life experience as well as imaginative excursions into other worlds. As children develop in their reading experiences different genres, plots and structures in picture books and novels offer insights into human values and issues that enable them to develop empathy, different levels of understanding and critical thinking. The majority of primary school teachers would never ignore the rich language and learning experiences that students derive from good literature. However the emphasis in the Australian Curriculum: English on the essential value of literature gives an imprimatur to what has been the practice of many teachers for decades.

In our research we found that teachers were either focusing on literature as the central theme of their unit, or integrating literature in their programs when the topic was focusing on a content area from Science or the Social Sciences. Digital technologies were used to extend many of the students' responses to literature. Several examples are referred to through this book but two specific cases are detailed here in Vignettes 8 and 9 where studies of literature in middle primary classes demonstrate the richness of learning experiences that can be incorporated with literature and digital technology.

VIGNETTE 8: 'NARRATIVES THROUGH FAIRYTALES'

This Year 3 class read and responded to a range of traditional and modern fairy tales. A specific focus was on different versions of Little Red Riding Hood and the way the wolf was represented in traditional and modern fairy tales. Some picture books used included *The Wolf's Story: What really happened to Little Red Riding Hood.* (Izhar, 2006), *The True Story of the Three Little Pigs by A. Wolf* (Scieszka & Smith, 1989) and *The Wolf* (Barbalet & Tanner, 1991). A non-fiction text about wolves was also read as a contrast of perspectives. Students developed their response to literature through various combinations of print, digital photography and video. Their understanding of the structure of a narrative, intertextuality and the ambiguities existing between the written and visual texts were enhanced as they compared traditional fairy stories with modern versions.

The range of responses included audio interviews or drama where students role-played different characters from the stories. Students responded with a variety of their own written narratives and other written forms 'in role' such as diary accounts, imaginative newspaper articles, recipes and postcards. These were all recorded on screen for others to see and comment on.

The teacher created interesting screen-based activities which were hyperlinked to files of different types of writing by students: journals written with students in the role of a wolf and written or oral procedures of recipes. Examples of these are shown in Figures 38 and 39

Groups of students wrote drama scripts that were performed, filmed and edited using Windows *Moviemaker*. For example students clicked on a particular character from the story shown on the screen in Figure 40. There was a hyperlink to videos of dramatisations of students in role, as shown in Figures 41 and 42, with one student as the interviewer and another student as the particular character in the story of *Little Red Riding Hood*.

By clicking on to any of the characters on the screen in Figure 40 students could view a video of two students role-playing a television interview with one student as the interviewer and the other students in the roles of Red Riding Hood or the Woodcutter, respectively. Figures 41 and 42 show screen shots from two of these interviews.

Such role-plays are not new but easier access to video technology, combined with IWB software, allows these performances to be saved and shown again to students in other classes or to parents. Similarly this role play allows for further development of students' oral language and imaginative recreation

Figure 38. Screen display with hyperlinks to students' journal entries from the point of view of a wolf

Figure 39. Screen display with hyperlinks to students' written or oral recipes

Figure 40. Screen display with hyperlinks to different videos of role-plays

as shown in the following example of dialogue between the interviewer and the 'Woodcutter'.

> Interviewer: Woodcutter, how did you know the wolf was in the house?
> Woodcutter: I heard screams – she was screaming very loudly and she could be heard a long way away.
> Interviewer: Do you live in the woods or outside the wood?
> Woodcutter: Outside the woods but I come into the woods of course – I'm a woodcutter.

These instances allow for students to be engaged in imaginative recreations and for other students to respond and learn from these. Such a wide range of activities develop student's response to literature in exciting ways, while building different levels of response and comprehension.

Vignette 9 shows another example of how teachers developed a rich learning experience by considering the use of narrators in fairy stories. The program developed students' critical responses by raising the whole issue of whether narrators are 'reliable' or 'unreliable', beginning with one of the same picture books referred to in Vignette 8, *The True Story of the Three Little Pigs by A. Wolf* (Scieszka & Smith, 1989).

Part of the process of claymation as used in Vignette 9, after making the clay figures, is to use stop motion animation, previously described in Chapter 2. Figure 43 shows an example of students going through the processes of stop motion animation to develop their claymations.

Figure 41. Video role-play of an Interviewer and Red Riding Hood.

Figure 42. Video role-play of an Interviewer and the Woodcutter.

VIGNETTE 9: THE 'UNRELIABLE NARRATOR'

This study by Year 2 students was planned to have students begin with considering the use of narrators in literature and to compare these with the way narrators were constructed in different stories and in other media such as television, film and computer games. Students were led to analyse and critique the use of different narrators, to consider how visual techniques, particularly colour and angles, were used in picture books and film. Traditional versions of fairy stories were read along with modern versions and the film *Hoodwinked* was viewed. Students developed written responses that showed their understanding of 'reliable' or 'unreliable' narrators. They gradually created their own written stories that were then developed as claymations.

Figure 43. The process of stop motion animation for claymation

While learning this technology engaged students, the study of literature entailed more than using new technology. Teachers raised students' awareness of the visual construction of meaning and point of view in images from the picture book, as shown in Figure 44. Here students are required to examine point of view by the use of angles in the three visual images shown in the book, *The Wolf's Story. What really happened to Little Red Riding Hood* (Izhar, 2006).

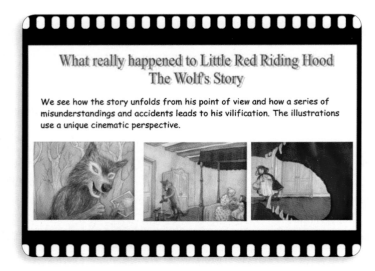

Figure 44. Raising students' awareness of how visuals construct point of view

To develop students' responses to reading along with different levels of comprehension, the teachers developed tasks that required students to use the 'four reading practices' or 'four roles of the reader' (Luke & Freebody, 1999) to encourage students' responses at different levels of comprehension. Figure 45 provides an example of how students' critical reading practice was extended by studying aspects of the movie *Hoodwinked*.

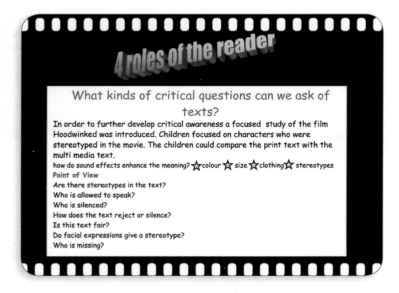

Figure 45. Building critical reading practices.

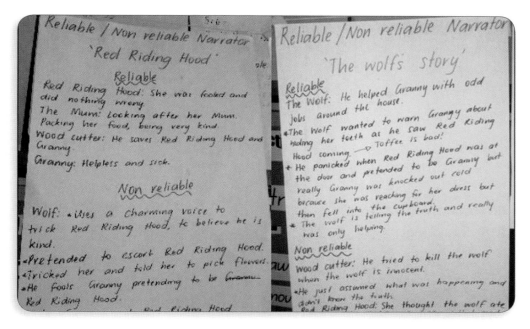

Figure 46. Students' understanding of different narrative perspectives

The students in this class were engaged in a multitude of literacy tasks which were essential in understanding the development of a narrative as told by an unreliable narrator. These tasks included film studies with a focus on unreliable narrators, discussion of the relationship between author and reader/viewer through an exploration of some elements of visual literacy. Figure 46 shows examples of some students' writing about the difference between reliable and unreliable narrators.

By focusing on traditional tales such as the story of *Little Red Riding Hood* and alternative versions of the text through the eyes of different characters, the teachers were able to engage students in critical literacy through questioning the validity of the narrator and by exploring alternative views from characters within the text. Students wrote joint constructions of narratives from the perspective of an unreliable narrator and created detailed storyboards for the sequencing and design of a claymation for their story. Students produced both a written version and a claymation version of their story. Figure 47 shows the titles of these stories developed by students while Figure 48 shows an example of the written version of the claymations.

The examples of students' writing and claymation illustrate the complementary relationship between traditional and new texts. In this program a claymation narrative was a culmination of the students' study of literature. While the storyboarding and claymation assisted students' understanding of narrative

Figure 47. Titles of claymation narratives.

The Bouncing Ball

One sunny day Tony and David decided to play with a bouncy ball outside their house on the grass.

First Tony said very angrily "it's my ball!" David said very angrily "it's my ball!"

Next, Tony had the ball, but David ran and grabbed the ball and angrily threw the ball back to Tony.

After that, Tony was sorry so they started to play roll the ball. Afterwards, Tony threw the ball to David and David head butted the ball and it was gone. They both tried to find the ball but they did not find it so they went to the green grass.

Finally they shook hand's and went inside their house.

By: Anthony 2Green

Figure 48. Students' written version of the claymation, 'The Bouncing Ball'

structures, students were led into a critical reading through comparing stereotypes and alternative representations. They examined the way specific visual effects constructed meaning in picture books and on screen. Teachers' comments on this program support the importance of the balance between traditional and new forms of learning:

COMMENT

Throughout the unit students explored the text structure of narratives. They produced storyboards, wrote scripts, created sets, props, and characters and produced a number of short animated films. Although the (claymation) movies were an integral part of the project, the development of children's knowledge, skills, values and attitudes provided the underlying foundation. These solid foundations enabled the students to produce high quality narratives. We believe the final product wouldn't have been successful without the initial development phase.

Response to literature online

Using online spaces to respond to literature is not a new idea and has been used for some time in the form of 'book raps' (Simpson, 2004). Book raps were designed for students to communicate online, initially through email, to students at other schools with activities structured around particular literary texts that both groups of students studied. As technology developed some teachers found software that enable sound and photography to be used in book raps but the facilities of digital technology with Web 2.0 now enable online communication to be used more easily and extensively.

Response to literature was an important focus for a Stage 2 teacher who used *VoiceThread* and a wiki to accompany students' work with the Harry Potter novels and a selection of other novels to suit the reading abilities of different students. Students were able to respond to aspects of the novels on *VoiceThread* as well as create their own narratives. Thus reading and writing were closely linked and occurring on screen as well in print, allowing others to see and comment at the same time. A tool such as *VoiceThread* allows for the specific aspects of students' progress over time to be assessed: their reading comprehension through their comments and interactions; their writing structures, spelling and punctuation; and their design ability and ICT proficiency.

These examples show that students can be engaged in literature in a range of exciting and varied ways and demonstrate that students' responses can be developed at a number of levels. A variety of both print and digital texts were produced to show students' understanding of literary narratives and these were complemented by role-play and drama.

THE POTENTIAL OF LITERATURE AND MULTIMODAL TEXTS

There is a wide range of literature available for children for all ages that can be used for both enjoyment and study. It has become accepted practice to use picture books in the teaching of reading for young students, as resources for rich language development and as models for writing in different styles. However their value as literature is important in the development of student's understanding of features of narratives and different literary genres. More complex picture books and graphic novels are also widely used for older students and offer multi-layered levels of meaning for developing student's understanding of and response to literature. Understanding the visual grammar of picture books adds to students' appreciation of the way meaning is constructed and assists students to understand the use of visuals in film and other screen-based media. In this way the use of picture books can provide the foundations for teaching about digital texts. Digital versions of picture books – whether as digital narratives, film or games – offer the opportunity for students to consider and compare the impact and purpose of different media and to consider the way meanings may be changed through the predominance of particular modes.

Similarly the study of novels can be supported by digital media that are part of normal communication for contemporary students. Availability of e:books, through the *Kindle* or *iPad*, may make the reading of novels more appealing for those students who are reluctant readers. Response to literature can be supported by digital narratives, internet search of author sites, fan fiction sites, fiction virtual worlds, reviews, written responses on screen, blogs, drama, photographs or movies. Online book clubs and responses through blogs and wikis can be established. If planned carefully and creatively students can still enjoy the magic of books along with complementary communication in digital media.

Rather than take the place of print-based texts, the examples presented in this chapter show that digital texts and use of technology simply added to the richness of the literature used in the teachers' programs. It is important for teachers to develop strategies for engaging students in the enjoyment and study of literature within the use of digital technologies. Within these new possibilities we need to find ways of still engaging students in silent, sustained and engaged reading of literature.

SUMMARY

Literature is an essential part of the curriculum and students can be involved in response to literature through varieties of digital technologies, carefully structured so that reading comprehension and writing abilities can be enhanced. Students can be led to:

- search the internet for digital or media versions of literature
- search for information about authors, the writing of particular books or the making of a picture book
- search for books by similar authors or books in the same genre
- participate in online chat about books, in wikis, blogs or fan fiction sites
- create their own written and digital texts or drama performances in response to literature.

CHAPTER 5
New texts in new spaces

INTRODUCTION

New literacy practices and new texts have evolved with the multimedia facilities of digital technology and several examples have been provided in the previous chapters. In addition, different texts were being adapted for classrooms using online and virtual spaces. With the increased accessibility of Web 2.0 social networking facilities, new texts such as blogs, wikis, or nings can be used, allowing for both synchronous and asynchronous interactive communication. There has been some debate about attempts to transfer such social networking practices to classroom learning situations. Recent studies (Hansford & Adlington, 2009) demonstrate the danger of teachers replicating students' use of blogs or wikis outside school. Hansford & Adlington emphasise the importance of teachers considering the potential, quality, social purpose and assessment of such texts.

In our research study, teachers were beginning to use aspects of social networking cautiously. In 2008 blogs were used in classes by two teachers and two used an online diary. In 2009 ten teachers were using online spaces more frequently and confidently to enhance the development of students' literacy. Those aspects of Web 2.0 that were used were the online diary *VoiceThread*, blogs and wikis. They were used for different purposes for students to:
- record their progress in learning in a diarised form that others could add to and comment on
- communicate their learning on a specific curriculum topic to others
- respond to literature
- improve writing in different forms (e.g. text types)

- further enhance their language proficiency
- comment on and critique other students' work.

Examples or these applications of social networking are discussed through this chapter with several vignettes presented.

WEAVING LEARNING THROUGH ONLINE DIARIES

Online diaries allow for students to record their learning progressively in a particular curriculum area with photographs, graphics and/or sound. Students can communicate with others as their writings and reflections are read and commented on by others. There is the potential for effective, independent learning to occur as students have to 'write out' their thinking into a form that is clear for others to read. Thus there is an authentic audience of their peers or teachers. As they read other students' work they see how others have expressed themselves so they may compare, reflect on and critique the writing of others as well as their own. Vignette 10 describes an application of this process.

VIGNETTE 10: USE OF THE ONLINE DIARY, VOICETHREAD

The *VoiceThread* site was used in two schools in 2008 for students to maintain an interactive record of their learning as described in the Vignettes 3 and 4 in the 'Digi-chicks' and 'Digi-vegies' units of work in Chapter 2. As students uploaded photos to diarise their learning, the images were supplemented with written text that supported their early reading and writing development. Other students could read and comment on these. In 2009 the same two teachers used *VoiceThread* for students to record their learning within the Science unit of work on 'On the move' that is discussed further in Chapter 6.

Figure 49 shows Year 1 students working in *VoiceThread* to write about the particular work they had completed that day about the chickens. Clay figures, that students had made to represent different stages of the chickens' growth, are shown on the shelf above the computer.

It is important to note that this use of the online diary was only one aspect of very rich units of work in both years and a compliment to the thorough, creative planning of the teachers. In each case students were exposed to rich concrete experiences around the topic, whether observing chickens, growing vegetables, or experimenting with the way things move. The online diaries in these cases were used to show the students' progressive learning about the Science content.

Figure 49. Using the online diary VoiceThread

BLOGS

The online diary feature of 'Weblogs' or blogs is appropriate where students are engaged in communicating information over time, particularly to cumulatively record and publish information that others may be interested in reading and responding to. Vignette 11 provides an example of the first time teachers used blogs in our research.

While blogging was not intended to be the main focus in the teachers' planning in this unit of work, it had a highly motivational impact on the older students in a similar way that younger students had been engaged with *VoiceThread*.

VIGNETTE 11: BLOGGING WITH CUBISM

In 2008 the teachers who worked on the unit on Picasso, described in Chapter 3, introduced students to blogging. Students posted entries onto a blog to comment on other students' cubist artwork that was photographed and available online, as shown in Figure 50. All the tasks required collaborative discussion, evaluation and critique in their class groups before their comments were posted on the blog. Students also wrote literary descriptions related to Picasso's art from the blue and rose period. These were posted on the blog for others to read and comment on.

Figure 50 A sample of the cubist artwork made available online

Both the processes involved in *VoiceThread* and blogging are similar Web 2.0 technologies and allow for the combination of different modes that may include written text, images, video, audio recording, sound effects and music. Even more so than the technological differences involved in processing multiple modes, these classroom adaptations of social networking allowed for ongoing communication and interaction between participants. Students were able to synchronously see other students' work, responses and opinions as they responded with their own.

Such online communication within the classrooms was establishing new social practices and extending the concept of talking and listening for learning. Students were responding to these modes of learning with enthusiasm. These examples of comments from the Years 5 and 6 students who, when asked, said they had all been on the social network sites, *Facebook* and *YouTube*.

COMMENTS
- With a blog you can have your own opinion.
- It's good because everyone can see what you say.
- It's more interesting for others to read.
- You learn from other people's work. [repeated by many students]
- You share.
- Everyone can see what you've done and it's your own opinion.
- You can see visual diagrams and colours.

- It's fun [repeated by many] because it's different from what we do everyday at school.
- It's fast.
- Everyone sees other people's work.
- Everyone sees all of them - if you are in one group in a class you only see the one.
- You won't forget - it's all up there.
- You can see quickly.
- You can see all the comments.

These students' comments emphasise the importance of 'seeing', that is, seeing by viewing through the use of the technology and seeing in terms of knowing and sharing with others. Such responses highlight the collaborative appeal of social networking practices. Viewing and connecting online becomes a component of reading and writing combined with talking and listening. Learning and literacy occur together in an integrated, holistic process, as shown in Chapter 2.

While it is not the role of schools to recreate multimedia experiences for their own sake, it is important to consider the way such technologies are able to be used to engage learners effectively. The researchers and teachers observed that students were highly motivated to respond and communicate with each other in this way and to collaborate within this medium of communication. Collaboration emerged as significant in many other ways throughout the study and is discussed further in Chapter 6.

Teachers were also pleased with the way students' responded to learning when the use of blogs was incorporated. Here is a comment from two teachers who worked together with their two classes.

COMMENT
The focus of the project at our school was to extend multimodal literacy through the use of a class blog. The children were encouraged to extend their critical analysis and collaboration skills through this process. As teachers we found that the use of Web 2.0 tools engaged and motivated the students by allowing them to write for a wider audience. We found that the use of digital technology enhanced the students' engagement and provided the opportunity for deeper learning to take place.

Blogging to improve language proficiency

More teachers introduced blogging in 2009 as blogs were being more widely used in schools. The following vignette is an example of one such experience.

VIGNETTE 12: BLOGGING WITH STUDENTS IN KOREA

In a Year 4 HSIE/SOSE program entitled 'Cooperative communities' students were interacting online with students from Korea. The majority of students in this school were from language backgrounds other than English and the teachers wished to extend the students' understanding of other communities as well as their local community. This initiative required a varied range of tasks that extended language and literacy strategies. Tasks included students writing factual descriptions of facilities within their school environment to post on the blog. In response, Korean students added factual descriptions of facilities within their school. Figure 51 shows the class blog page while Figure 52 is an example from an early entry on the blog as a student introduces aspects of an Australian classroom to Korean readers.

Through this blogging, a number of literacy skills were developed. These skills included the social protocols of students introducing themselves, developing an understanding of formal and informal language registers, knowledge of the difference between posts and comments, summarising, the ability to read and interpret other students' texts, and to select effective descriptive language appropriate to a particular audience.

Figure 51. A class blog page

Figure 52. A blog entry to Korean students

The Australian students made episodic videos of aspects of their school life that they uploaded onto the blog for the Korean students to view. These episodes included students filming and commenting on the physical features of their school (e.g. playground, school office and classrooms) as well as interviews with different members of staff to discuss their role in the school (e.g. office assistant, librarian, teacher). This incorporation of digital technology enabled and motivated students, who were mostly from language backgrounds other than English, to extend their use of oral as well as written language for effective communication to an audience of students in another country.

Blogs can be used in a variety of ways. While the program described in Vignette 12 was focusing on students' oral and written language development Vignette 13 shows an example of teachers using blogs specifically to improve students' writing ability.

In their concern for improving the quality of students' writing, the teachers considered that 'blogging would motivate students who did not appear to see the importance of producing quality work for an audience'. Students kept a separate journal to record their reflections on blogging and whether they thought it was improving the quality of their writing. The blogs were placed on the class home page, thus emphasising the importance of producing a product that others would view.

As a further innovation to foster students' evaluative skills, teachers gave students criteria for assessing writing. The teachers reported that this use of blogging motivated students to improve both their reading and writing as they were learning to re-evaluate their work through seeing the work of others. Students were engaged in aspects of critical practice in that they were required to read, comment on and evaluate posts made by other students.

It was apparent that students were very motivated to write and communicate online and teachers commented that these tasks were encouraging those students

VIGNETTE 13: BLOGGING TO IMPROVE WRITING ABILITY

In two upper primary classes in the one school, students were motivated to develop their writing ability through blogging. Year 5 focused on narrative writing while Year 6 focused on writing expositions that would lead into debating. The specific structure and language of each of these text types was taught at different stages along with emphasis on the importance of an audience. Students' writing incorporated links with images, music and research and students commented on and critiqued each other's work.

who would often be unwilling or less able with their written work. A teacher's comment is a pertinent observation on the way her class was motivated to read and write through the construction of their blog.

COMMENT

The blog ... was a rich opportunity to develop the students' skills in reading and viewing a text. The blog was a text that the students had created themselves. This ownership provided a motivation to read that could not be recreated using any teacher-created or commercial text.

WIKISPACES

Wikis have become a popular online multi-authoring tool and were used by several teachers to allow for students to collaborate in their writing and to post comments about their learning. Many teachers used the free *Wikispaces* software while others used the *Wetpaint* site.

Vignette 14 details one teacher's use of a wiki for writing description.

VIGNETTE 14: AN IGLOO FOR SHELTER

A Year 1 teacher used wikis to improve students' writing as well as their understanding of the Science and Technology topic of 'The Need for Shelter'. Students presented descriptions of different types of shelters and they were required to develop their own photo story of a shelter that they presented to the class with recorded commentary with music and/or sound effects. This text was uploaded onto the wiki. Figure 53 shows where a student produced a photo story of an Igloo. The student accompanied this photo story with a PowerPoint that described Igloos using focus questions provided by the teacher, e.g. *Who uses the shelter? How is it built? What is it made of? and Where can it be found?* The students' photo stories were saved through the IWB software that others could access.

The teacher then expanded students' descriptions into expositions by having them learn how to express an opinion and support it with evidence. In this case students had to respond to questions about the nature of shelters within the wiki. For example one question the students had to discuss was: *Are spider webs shelters?* This task required students to understand exactly what a shelter was, to research the features of spider webs and to decide on their opinion. They posted their

Figure 53. A Year 1 student's photo story of a shelter

opinion on the wiki and commented on other students' postings. Thus at this young age students were engaged in critical thinking and were required to express their opinion within a discussion that was respectful of other students' opinions as well as use appropriate sentence structure, vocabulary and spelling. The following presents examples of students' comments on their learning.

COMMENTS
- The wiki space is my favourite because its fun and we get to talk to each other on it.
- It's good to do the wiki space at home because its like homework but not because its fun.
- Adding pictures and writing on my wiki is cool.
- I like using the camera because it make me feel like a grown up on holidays.
- Its fun going on the wiki space and making comments on our teacher's questions.

The teacher commented on the benefits of using the wiki for extending the literacy skills of the students:

COMMENT
Students who are usually very slow to start, and who rarely finish anything, were very eager and keen to produce their work on the computer. I think the use of different modes of media within the classroom really enhanced individual learning styles as students were allowed to present their work in a style that best suited them.

> The Wiki Space was the most successful aspect. This not only enhanced learning but it enhanced the students' attitude to literacy.

In another creative approach that engaged young students, a Year 2 teacher combined the content and skills of three content areas that were usually taught separately. The program is summarised in Vignette 15.

VIGNETTE 15 INVESTIGATING 'OLDEN DAYS'

The writing of a procedural text for English was taught with the HSIE/SOSE theme of 'Olden Days' and combined with the Science and Technology topic of 'Toys', particularly those that could be pushed or pulled. Part of this program required students to research toys used by children in the past, make them and photograph the procedure they used. They were required to use drawing, photographs and words for their procedure. As they made the toy they had to take a picture of each step, describe each step with an action verb and then film each step. The students recorded the procedure on *iPod*s through a podcast and then transferred these spoken 'procedures' into written and video form on to a class wiki site. Other students were able to add to these wikis.

Figure 54 shows the guidelines displayed by the teacher and students engaged in the process.

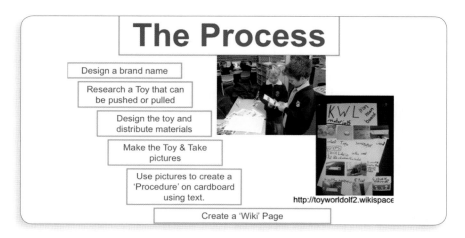

Figure 54. Different stages of learning and literacy that were recorded on a wiki

The detail required in each of the programs described in Vignettes 14 and 15 was quite cognitively demanding for young students, particularly the process of demonstrating a procedure, with written text, photographs and audio instruction, for other students to make toys and to comment on the procedures. These initiatives demonstrate that teachers can use the features of social networking to further develop students' thinking and writing abilities.

Observation and discussion with students provided some insights into why these tasks, that incorporated social networking practices, engaged students so much. Students in different classes were asked about what they liked about wikis or blogs and their comments were similar across ages and schools. Some representative examples of students' responses are shown here.

COMMENTS
You get to see other people's work.
You get ideas from seeing other people's work.
Everyone knows what everyone else is doing.
You can comment on what others have done.
Other people can give you more ideas on your work.

Once again, these comments highlight students' positive responses to the participatory nature of online literacy practices where reading and writing are interrelated processes. Interchange of comments and ideas occur, offering a vibrant learning environment. When asked about why writing in blogs or wikis was more enjoyable than writing in their books, students commented that when they usually completed a piece of writing in their books or on paper, their work was 'finished' whereas, with wikis or blogs, they were able to read and comment on their peers' work. They also commented that they were conscious of the need to keep improving on their work because others would be reading it.

Teachers commented that they were able to build on students' written language successfully through having students write in wikis or blogs and that students were enhancing their writing with design. Students used photos, other images or graphics, and were very concerned with the layout, use of font and arrangement of their work on the screen knowing that others would view and critique their work. There was a more conscious awareness of the appropriate language, style and structure, along with correct grammar, spelling and punctuation that should be used to suit the text they were producing for their audience.

REFLECTION

What makes these texts 'new' compared with previous texts developed by students in traditional classrooms? As you think about the examples presented consider these suggestions about the way texts in social networking spaces are different.

- They occur online, in virtual spaces, rather than on paper or in recordable files such as video, CD, or CD-Rom.
- The work is not written as a single text for a teacher to comment on and assess but is created to show others and to communicate with others.
- They can be progressive, rather than a final piece of writing, that can improve, be altered by others, show reflection and critique.
- Some, for example a class blog or wiki, require collaboration to produce so planning and design are important.
- They focus on presentation: presentation of the self, or a group, an idea or comment on events.
- The way this 'self', or 'selves' in a group, is presented is a crucial aspect of these texts.
- What do these differences mean for literacy? How can we describe literacy in these practices? What is the function of reading and writing?

The examples presented in this chapter were teachers' initial excursions into the application of some social networking practices for classroom literacy learning. Teachers were cautious in ensuring the privacy of class blogs or wikis and established clear protocols for students to adhere to, especially to ensure that participation in these spaces was positive and constructive. Students were informed about the importance of privacy and the dangers of online stalking or bullying. While there were positive results from students and teachers from their engagement with online communication it is important to acknowledge that there are many challenges that schools face in deciding on the extent of participation that can occur.

SUMMARY

The potentials of social networking used in the research allowed students to:
- record their learning
- see other students' work and respond in a constructive way
- write in different styles for different purposes
- augment their writing with photos, sound, drawings or video.

Both teachers' and students' responses to these preliminary classroom applications of social networking produced a more collaborative and participatory culture in the classes. Further evidence and research is needed to devise appropriate pedagogy and protocols.

CHAPTER 6
New classroom dynamics

INTRODUCTION

The classroom literacy practices presented in this book illustrate the way many teachers responded to the challenges of new technologies and incorporated them in different ways, depending on the literacy learning needs of their students and the resources they had available. The way teachers planned required students to work together, often with teachers learning new digital technology or aspects of the technology that they had not used before. Teachers commented that this process in itself changed their relationship with students whose confidence was boosted by being able to assist teachers or peers. There were several instances where students, who normally did not 'achieve' at traditional reading and writing tasks, became leaders in demonstrating technological applications. For example one Year 3 student led his peers in using *Garage Band* for editing digital texts with sound and music, while a student in a Year 5 class became an expert at demonstrating the features of an IWB.

Collaboration between students was essential as they worked together to produce digital products within these new communication contexts. Teachers commented that although collaboration had always been important in group tasks with pen and paper, the digital environment required more manipulation of technical aspects with peer tutoring and evaluation as students worked together to produce a final product. Teachers' excursions into some aspects of social networking indicated that students were highly motivated to communicate in this medium, observing and commenting on their peers' work.

The social dynamics of classrooms were clearly changing as students and teachers were becoming problem solvers together. The collaborative and participatory approaches engendered more talking and listening and this talking around and about learning impacted on both student's metacognitive strategies and metalinguistic use of language

Implications of these changes are discussed in this chapter.

NEW PATTERNS OF INTERACTION FOR LANGUAGE LEARNING

Within the research teachers showed they were aware of the need to develop students' language proficiency for effective literacy development. As many of the schools were in dense metropolitan areas of Sydney there were large numbers of students from language backgrounds other than English in several of the classes. The holistic, continuous nature of learning, referred to in previous chapters, meant that the oral and written language of students was developed along a continuum, similar to the principles of the 'mode continuum' (Jones, 1996 p.13) that for some decades has been guiding the teaching of language and literacy, particularly for English as an Additional Language (EAL) learners. The concept of the mode continuum provides a useful focus for teachers to understand particularly how oral and written language can be developed from 'spoken like' to more 'written like' language, and from communicative to more academic language proficiency (Cummins, 1984). Vignette 16 refers to the way this continuum was developed within the Kindergarten unit 'On the Move'.

Figure 55. Students working a pulley

VIGNETTE 16: ON THE MOVE

Two teachers combined their Kindergarten classes for students to investigate basic principles of movement by experimenting with a large range of objects that moved. While students used and seemed to be 'playing' with various items the teachers carefully modelled different vocabulary and language structures for the students. For example, structures such as: *What can you do to make that move? Do you have to push it or turn it?* were assisting the language development of these young students, the majority of whom come from home language backgrounds other than English. Learning for these students involved experimenting with concrete materials that offered a continual stimulus to explore and investigate what objects would move or not, how they moved and what made them move, as shown in Figures 55, 56 and 57 where students are shown experimenting with different moving objects, e.g. pulleys, marbles in a winding track and bicycle wheels.

Figure 56. Students experimenting with the way marbles roll on a track

Flip cameras were used to record students learning. The videos were played back to the students and discussed with further feedback from the teachers. Thus oral language was constantly being extended through teacher modelling. Varieties of written language were modelled in visual displays around the room and combined with digital technology for students to record their learning and to assist students' early reading and writing, as shown in Figure 58.

Figure 57. Using pulleys for construction

Figure 58. The classroom diary on a display board – written accounts, drawings and photographs by students and teachers

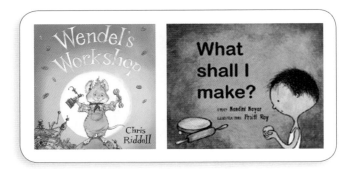

Figure 59. Literature and non-fiction integrated into Science learning

Internet sites including *YouTube* and *Google Earth*, were accessed. The written explanations about how things moved were developed after the students talked through many experiences. These experiences were recorded with the use of the webcam, digital microscopes, *Flip* cameras, *2Simple* software and posted on *VoiceThread*.

The reading of literature and information texts was integrated, as shown in the texts used in Figure 59.

To build on their learning about movement students watched a video of the making of a Billy Cart and then, in pairs, were required to design their own Billy Cart from clay with a track for the carts to move on. These movements of the cart

Figure 60. An image from the claymation of Ben and Aaron's Billy Cart Race Track

around the track were then photographed to produce a claymation. To achieve the final product of a claymation the students had to explain the movements of the carts orally and include written text on the screen. Figure 60 presents an image from Ben and Aaron's claymation and an extract of the language they used in their recording to accompany the claymation is given below it.

Extract from Ben and Aaron's Billy Cart Race Track.

The billy cart is pushed. The billy cart will go down the ramp and the bumpy ground really quickly because it is steep. Then the billy cart will go through two tunnels that are near each other. After that it will go around onto the blue track to take a short cut. The billy cart goes up and over the bridge because there are crocodiles in the water under the bridge. When it gets to the yellow track it quickly needs to turn round and go to the end. Finally the billy cart gets under the tunnel because there isn't a ramp and the billy cart wheels run out of energy. It it doesn't stop it will go up the ramp and down. The end.

This oral account was accompanied by music and text on the screen. It is evident that students were learning language for sequencing, description, procedure and cause and effect. This language was supporting students' learning about movement and energy for Science.

· ·

REFLECTION

Consider the following learning and literacy needed for Kindergarten students to produce this claymation. Could you assess students' literacy and learning outcomes from students':
* understanding about the Science topic of movement?
* language related to the content area of movement?
* sequential structure of the explanation?
* cause and effect language required for an explanation?
* use of language and grammar appropriate to the text?

Can you identify the amount of teacher scaffolding that occurred for these student to be able to produce this claymation?

· ·

The progressive, cohesive nature of the teachers' planning allowed for the students' language learning to develop within a continuum so that the students moved from oral to written language structures and were gradually gaining more proficiency in these. Even more so the investigative, collaborative nature of learning was ensuring that students' were engaged in exploratory talk, discussion, argument and reflective dialogue.

As previously shown in the program referred to in Vignette 12, Chapter 5, opportunities for language development were carefully structured and scaffolded for the Year 4 students within their program, 'Collaborative communities'. The teachers explained that they had planned to develop 'substantial communication opportunities' through the online blog for the Australian students to communicate with the Korean students. Students had to learn a number of language structures while specifically focusing on the language for factual descriptions. As well as learning the technology of a blog itself, they had to plan appropriate written language for their posts and comments, adjust their written language to communicate in clear English to the Korean students who understandably were struggling to communicate in English, and to rehearse spoken language for their videos which provided commentary and descriptions of their school. Students were conscious of the need for clear language of description and of explanation, with occasional comments, along with the projection of their voice for the Korean audience. Questioning strategies were modelled by the teachers to assist students' own questions for their investigations, interviews with members of the school community and online discussions. Students were required to plan their script and enunciate it clearly with appropriate facial expression and body language. They planned the video segments in their groups with an understanding of the use of camera shots and angles, as well as maintaining film continuity

This example further highlights that a continuum can be developed with language learning, particularly for young language learners. Specific experiences can be planned for students' learning with teachers consciously modelling spoken language that is related to new concepts, new vocabulary and appropriate grammatical structures. Examples of this language can then be produced in written structures of sentences and whole texts on paper, charts or screen. If these written products are augmented with photos and audio to produce different types of digital texts, digital communication is augmenting the interrelationship between modes of language and other semiotic systems.

Two teachers from another school commented that, although they had developed many effective reading and writing activities for their Year 4 students, they considered the most progress was made in students' talking and listening. This comment from the teachers demonstrates their observations of the students' oracy development through their program:

COMMENT

Initially, the children were self-conscious and quite nervous
when using oral language in a more formal setting, for example
when interviewing each other. Having an audience inhibited them
as did being videoed by one of their peers. Gradually they overcame
this and began to enjoy performing. As their enjoyment grew so
did their confidence and, as a result, the quality of what they
produced. The students saw the benefits of being able to play back
their videos instantaneously to analyse them and improve their
subsequent recordings.

Many similar examples could be given from the teachers' programs. Problem-solving investigations fostered oral language being extended with metacognition and metalinguistic development. For example in the 'Light Fantastic' program (Chapter 3), students were given focus questions to comment on at the beginning and the end of the project. These questions were related to how light helps us to see; how an eye works; how light travels; how different materials affect how light travels; how light travels around corners; and how light creates shadows. Student talked through their learning at different stages as they were led to investigate, answer the questions and use the correct technical language related to light (*transparent, translucent, opaque*) or the structure of the eye (*iris, retina*).

Language interaction was occurring through different levels of collaboration, which was a principal feature of students' approach to learning. Web 2.0 technologies foster communication, participation, information sharing and problem solving. If planned effectively, classroom tasks can require students to use more demanding levels of oral language with more cognitively demanding tasks. With teachers using these approaches in many programs, the nature of collaboration was further enhanced. A comment by two other teachers is an insightful reflection on the changes that were occurring in their classroom:

COMMENT

A new language occurred through the integration of new
technologies and through the analysis and creation of a range
of multimodal texts. Communication became more powerful and
purposeful for the students.

Students responded to the challenges of new learning environments. They showed that they were able to help each other learn and work towards final products, whether it was learning to use effective camera angles or editing for a video or producing a digital text on screen incorporating effective text, visuals and graphics. In two schools teachers applied the 'think, pair, share' strategy with groups of three students so that students could learn different aspects of technology and teach others. In another school the teachers used a strategy where they taught the blogging process to two students using the blogging website 21classes.com. When students were comfortable they taught another two students. These, in turn, taught another two students. While the teachers monitored the overall process, students became 'experts' thus becoming independent learners and problem solvers. The development of oral language proficiency was an essential outcome of this collaborative approach to learning.

NEW WAYS OF COLLABORATING

Digital communication has had a significant impact on the social climate among students and has challenged traditional role expectations of classroom teachers. Along with the increase in student engagement through the use of digital technologies, all teachers involved in these case studies commented on the collaborative, outcome-focused group dynamics, which were highly driven by the need to produce quality work for a specific audience. Through digital technology-based tasks, students were openly willing to provide peer support, offer constructive, critical feedback and, most remarkably, positively accept this feedback and alter their work accordingly. Due to an awareness of immediate support from peers and the capacity for errors to be amended effortlessly through the use of digital technologies, students became risk takers. As a result many teachers commented that all students, even those who were often reserved and who rarely contributed, were willing to participate.

Notably, with this significant change in the way students were engaging with each other through digital communication, the role of the classroom teacher shifted from leader to partner. Teachers commented on the need to collaboratively work with their students to direct the teaching program based primarily upon student need and interest. One teacher commented that she had become a *facilitator*.

> ### COMMENT
> ...a member of the community of 'knowledge workers' where each member is both a teacher and a learner. As a result, all learners are deeply connected to learning and knowledge development.

Along with the collaborative nature of communication that occurred with online diaries and blogging activities, collaboration occurred throughout all the case studies as students worked together. Once again, both researchers and teachers observed the nature of this collaboration as different from previous ways that students had worked in group activities. Group work and cooperative learning have existed in education for several decades but we considered that there were different dynamics occurring in students' interactions with each other and with the tasks.

Although these differences cannot be quantitatively proven, there is evidence from the research to show that students' cooperation with others had taken on a distinct profile. This profile was evident in students having a purpose, usually to create a digital or multimedia text to be communicated to an audience. To achieve this purpose they assisted each other, negotiated, supported and critiqued their peers' work to create a final product for an audience.

This profile of collaboration was undoubtedly linked to the affordances of digital communication technologies. Students were highly motivated to work together, not only to use the technology, but also to create products that were evidence of their learning in the particular curriculum area. One teacher's comment sums up the motivation of students as they wrote and produced print and digital texts.

TEACHER COMMENT
We found that students were more engaged in the writing process due to the fact that there was a motivating goal for them to achieve collaboratively.

A NEW SOCIAL PROFILE

Talking, listening and working collaboratively were major features that contributed to students' learning within the programs developed by teachers. This feature was strongly reinforced by students' own comments. It was evident that students were motivated to work together and were learning from each other. Students' comments and teachers' observations affirmed that students were engaged when they all saw each other's work and shared ideas, particularly in the blogging process. It became apparent that the incorporation of digital technology was changing the way teachers could utilise the oracy of students to develop literacy learning. The range of activities that occurred meant that talking, listening and learning were linked to the interaction with digital technologies and, as already shown, created a different social profile of collaboration between students within the classroom.

It is difficult to determine whether this social profile of collaboration is directly related to the increase of social networking practices of Web 2.0, along with the overall changes in communication with digital technologies. Research into aspects of social networking is at preliminary stages and not able to proceed as fast as the phenomenon itself. There is evidence, however, to show that social networking is more interactive and participatory, and that the nature of literacy practices in online or virtual environments are shaping identities differently (Coiro et al, 2008). The data from this research show that interactive and participatory features enabled students to engage enthusiastically in learning. Perhaps students were responding to modes of learning and communication that they are encountering outside school. The question of students adapting their identities to suit different online practices or virtual worlds was not evident within this study with primary school students. Other research (Lewis & Farbos, 2005) is indicating that the issue of identity is an important consideration for future pedagogy that uses social networking practices.

While much more research is needed to consider classroom implications, it was evident that the social features of digital communication technologies were intertwined with students' motivation and engagement in learning.

SUMMARY

Classroom dynamics were changing with the incorporation of digital communication technologies. These included:
• students working in more collaborative ways
• students and teachers learning together
• more self-directed, independent learning
• more opportunities for language to be used for learning within problem solving and collaborative tasks

The social profile of classrooms was seen to be changing as a result of the more interactive and participatory nature of teachers programming differently. Features of technology encouraged students to work together either in response to particular texts or to develop new texts.

CHAPTER 7

New ways of teaching: implications of this research for literacy education

INTRODUCTION

The three streams of language, literature and literacy proposed by the Australian Curriculum: English require teachers to integrate the teaching of the proficiencies required for these three streams. Further, teachers need to be able to teach separate skills and strategies detailed for each of the streams, as appropriate to the Year level. The multimodal language and literacy experiences, described in the previous chapters, innately lend themselves towards more holistic learning. Thus the research shows that the three streams of the curriculum can be interrelated with aspects of language, literature and literacy occurring cohesively as well as allowing for focus on specific skills.

Rather than teaching segmented lessons, in this research study, many teachers planned so that essential skills were required within the tasks. At the same time the explicit teaching of skills continued to occur within these programs progressively. As has been shown, teachers modelled and scaffolded language and literacy strategies throughout the learning process. There was a cyclical process of talking and listening, reading and writing where students were gradually engaged in more critical, evaluative conversation with the intent of producing work on their learning (either digitally or on paper) for a specific audience.

There are many implications and challenges for the way this research offers insight for teachers to consider the integration of digital communications technology and the implementation of the Australian Curriculum: English. Some of these implications and challenges, discussed in this chapter, are:

- literature, and the rich world of books, can be experienced within a multimodal literacy environment
- student learning can be engaged through integration of literacy with other curriculum areas
- assessment can be more individualised and rigorous
- the importance of an understanding of design within new literacy practices.
- new descriptors of talking, listening, reading and writing need to be considered within digital communication environments

THE IMPORTANCE OF LITERATURE IN THE CURRICULUM

As detailed in Chapter 4, literature is an essential basis for an English curriculum across all ages. The research showed that many creative responses to literature could be developed using both print and digital technologies. At the same time, much of the literature used was picture books with only one class focusing on the study of novels. This may have been because of the focus on other curriculum areas but there is a need for teachers to develop ways of using novels in the middle and upper primary classes and to motivate students to read widely. As the survey in Chapter 1 revealed, older students were less interested in reading novels. This is an important challenge – How do we engage students of today in close reading of literature? Digital technologies, particularly gaming and social networking, are of course competing with the reading of books. We need to find ways to complement literature study with digital texts and resources. Some examples have been shown in this book but much more work is needed in this area.

ENGAGING STUDENT LEARNING THROUGH INTEGRATION

Classroom examples have been presented throughout this book, and particularly in Chapter 2, to show that teachers were developing a cyclic process of building the field for students' learning about particular topics in content areas, leading students to research and to produce final products of their learning. This cyclic process was recursive and occurred over several weeks so that specific language, reading and writing skills could be developed gradually with the content area being the learning context for literacy. While the concept of integration has existed in education for some time, the incorporation of digital technologies enabled a more holistic process of literacy strategies and learning. An overall finding was that digital technologies were integrated in purposeful and innovative ways thus ensuring a richness of learning when literacy activities, modes and texts were connected.

ASSESSMENT: MORE INDIVIDUALISED AND MORE RIGOROUS

There is always a tension between national assessment criteria and more individualised, formative assessment of students over time. Summative assessment from standardised tests has the advantage of showing the performance of a student in comparison to others of the same age locally or nationally. Formative assessment allows teachers to develop a full profile of individual students' strengths and aspects that need attention. Both forms of assessment are valuable and in this research it became evident that the incorporation of digital technologies allowed teachers to maintain evidence of students' work progressively. Technology provides the opportunity for a profile of individual students to be recorded and compared over time.

Records of work, particularly digital products, were saved and available for showing to parents and to compare students' progress at different stages within a unit of work or over a longer time. Students' written work online, whether wikis or blogs, could be assessed at text, sentence and word level along with spelling and punctuation. Similarly different levels of reading comprehension could be assessed through examining students' responses in digital forms to tasks. As evidenced through the range of integrated programs presented through this book, content area learning and ICT skills could also be assessed within the same tasks. Furthermore, different creative, artistic and technical abilities emerged to reveal talents of students who do not usually succeed at traditional reading and writing tasks.

Mainly, through the types of programs observed, students worked in small groups with an expectation to share their knowledge and their digital technology skills in order to design, and then produce, for a real audience through reading and writing. As groups reached new challenges they were expected to negotiate, challenge, question and evaluate the practices of their peers. In turn, this encouraged reflective talking and listening in order to reconsider their ideas. These situations provide a range of opportunities for teachers to assess aspects of students' learning and thinking as well as speaking and listening skills. For example in the program 'Light Fantastic' (Chapter 3), teachers were able to assess students' ongoing learning through the program as students were required to record their learning in the 'diary room' either in books or with *Flip* cameras. Figure 61 shows a photograph of the chart that teachers had on display in the room to help students understand the process of their learning. The teachers devised the students' progression through learning as a reflective cycle.

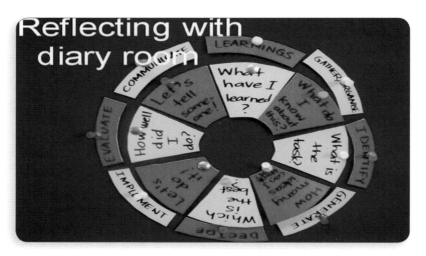

Figure 61. The learning and reflecting cycle with 'Light'

The diagram summarises a cohesive process where students investigated specific questions about light, recorded their learning in written and digital forms, reflected on this learning and produced a multimedia text that demonstrated their learning. This learning cycle was used as an evaluation for students to reflect on their learning throughout the program. It was a guide and scaffold at different stages, requiring students' ongoing reflection during their program and at the end. Student reflection was an important aspect of this scientific investigation and, as an interesting innovation, teachers had students record their reflections with the *Flip* cameras. These digital records provided a range of data that could be accessed to assess student outcomes.

Assessment became a more continuous process as evidence of students' development over time was recorded. This approach allowed for formative assessment of specific aspects of language, literacy and learning, including new skills and strategies needed for communicating in a digital environment.

Assessment should inform the way teachers program to assess the learning that has been achieved through what has been taught, whether the outcomes result in print or digital products. Authentic assessment includes the observation and recording of the processes students go through, whatever the final product. Thus teacher planning, evaluation and reflection are crucial. Teachers who were involved in this research became very reflective of their own teaching. Figure 62 is one of many examples of teacher reflection on their program, highlighting

DIFFICULTIES AND SUCCESSES

- The project worked well overall and there has been a real improvement in the quality of writing as well as the enthusiasm for writing.
- On the computers, we matched students with partners of similar reading ability. This worked really well.
- The talking and listening activities increased the students' confidence with the language of the topic.
- At times, students had to write directoy onto the computer without a draft. Of their recount. However students were more confident that they knew the topic and used their own words rather than trying to cut and paste.
- Students were able to link a classmate with a convict story whcih regularly assisted recall of facts. Students who preferred the literary style of recount had the opportunity to write a lette.
- Children had opportunities to write a biography of Captain Cook, a factual recpouont of The Rocks excursion and create a movie about a convict. Students were proud of their computer presentations and could evaluate each other's efforts.
- It highlighted the fact that some students could not match images to text and this will be a focus in the future.

Figure 62. Teacher evaluation of the Year 4 program, 'British Colonisation'

areas that succeeded and that were difficult, showing that this reflection would inform future programming.

This type of reflection by teachers has an impact on their attitude to assessment and informs their teaching.

In programming their units of work, teachers planned to incorporate some form of digital technology for literacy learning. Thus they also planned that students work with digital technology would be assessed. Through the implementations of the programs more possibilities for assessment with digital technology became evident. It was not the use of technology itself that was making teachers reflect on their teaching and assessment of students but rather the fact that teachers were empowered by becoming partners in research to rethink their approach to teaching and learning. Many of the teachers found they had more scope for assessment and are continuing to embed the assessment of literacy with the assessment of technology use.

THE IMPORTANCE OF DESIGN WITHIN NEW LITERACY PRACTICES.

Design emerged as an integral component of writing and producing texts. As students were producing multimodal texts, such as a video or a claymation, they had to consider and understand features of design such as layout, composition, use of text and image or graphics – including aspects such as colour, size, medium, angles – and the way these would suit a specific audience.

Design is emerging as a significant element of being literate in digital communication environments (Kalantzis & Cope, 2005; Healy, 2008) and the Australian National Curriculum makes these notions explicit as well. This research confirmed the integral nature of design. While students in all of the programs were involved in a range of writing activities around relevant text types, students extended this writing into published work, augmented by photos and graphics. Aided by digital software programs a great deal of the students' work was developed into media products such as videos, online websites, slide shows or claymations. Students were engaged in learning about the structure and language for writing particular text types as well as the structure and design of words with other modes of image or sound. Students were learning the metalanguage of written structures and grammar along with the metalanguage of digital texts.

Design has been shown to be an integral process with multimodal literacy. We need further investigation about how much students need to understand and deconstruct the design and language of a visual or digital text to understand its meaning and purpose. Similarly, we need to consider what teachers and students need to know about design to produce a visual or digital text for a particular audience and whether this design process is similar to or different from the way design is used in other curriculum areas, particularly Science and the Visual Arts.

REFLECTION

A further challenge is to consider how the use of design can be integrated with the teaching of the writing of text types and their specific structure, language and grammar when producing multimodal texts. Currently there are effective established approaches to teaching writing through different text types. It will be essential for similar models and scaffolds to be developed for onscreen writing so that writing in online modes, particularly blogs, is not reduced to 'speech written down' with simple linguistic constructions. Students need to be able to use varied and complex language structures in digital environments.

Teachers in this project provided scaffolds for the type of writing students were producing on screen and maintained a continuum between writing on paper and on screen. Such an approach will be needed for students to understand ways of using the appropriate spoken and written modes of language in online texts.

NEW DESCRIPTORS OF TALKING, LISTENING, READING AND WRITING

Multimodal literacy represents the interdependency and fluidity between language and literacy functions. Analysis of the classroom data showed that talking and listening often led to, or evolved from, reading or writing tasks. Reading occurred on screen as well as on paper so that the navigation of different screens and pathways was a different process from the more linear reading of printed texts. In most of the programs teachers integrated literacy within different curriculum areas and these KLAs varied between Science, HSIE/SOSE and Creative Arts. The focus on literacy within these curriculum subjects ensured that students needed to build their knowledge of the field, or content knowledge, in their understanding of concepts, development of vocabulary knowledge, and ways of using language structures in spoken and written forms to observe, describe, report, explain or discuss key aspects of knowledge. Thus, as has been shown, there was the continual merging of learning experiences with print and digital materials, along with talking, listening, reading and writing and producing texts for real purposes.

Use and interaction with digital technology was the extra layer that we explored within all the language and literacy criteria in the consideration of how digital communication impacted on students' literacy learning. Data was analysed to examine what differences occurred in literacy practices within the use of digital technology and digital texts. These findings led to a definition of multimodal literacy as entailing the interrelationship and coherence between different modes (Walsh, 2008; 2010). Thus within the consideration of specific aspects of talking, listening, reading and writing we examined the exact ways aspects of literacy were multimodal; how this multimodality occurred within students' learning; and how teachers' pedagogy had enabled this learning to occur. Through this analysis we considered whether the use and production of digital texts has changed the nature of literacy itself, and to what extent pedagogy needs to be redesigned for such changes.

New, additional descriptions of language and literacy are proposed here. Specific terms are listed within each criterion to demonstrate those practices that usually occur. These descriptors are suggested to show further practices that are occurring with digital communication. These terms are not definitive and, with the changing nature of new technologies, are a 'work in progress'. They are an attempt to demonstrate how this research showed that literacy practices are developing further dimensions within new communication environments. The next three sections propose a further consideration of reading, writing, talking and listening by adding new descriptors to existing descriptions.

Reading in print and multimodal contexts

Reading entailed students being involved in shared, modelled and independent reading with various phonics, word recognition and vocabulary activities appropriate to their age. It also involved students responding at different levels of literal, inferential, analytical and critical understanding with information books and literature. However many of these activities were with digital texts such as internet sites. Students interacted with texts and with others as they researched information in books or on screen. On-screen reading incorporates multisensory activities such as searching, viewing, browsing, scrolling and navigating together with the clicking and scrolling of a mouse. As reading and viewing are often interchangeable processes, additional descriptors of reading should include aspects such as browsing, scrolling, searching, navigating and hyperlinking. It is important to note, however, that students also need to be able to interpret, analyse and critique levels of meaning in digital and web-based texts.

Writing in print and multimodal contexts

Writing involved all students writing one or more text type on paper and using the appropriate structure and grammar for these. This process then led to students composing, planning, designing and producing texts on paper to be transformed into digital or multimedia texts on screen. On screen writing usually became part of a designed product for an audience e.g. a poster or a pamphlet, website, slide show or a multimedia text such as a movie, with graphics, animation and sound. Students developed skills for evaluating and critiquing their own and their peers' work as they considered the purpose of their text and its appropriateness for its audience. Thus additional descriptors of of writing should incorporate terms such as composing, creating, designing, evaluating, planning, producing, and transforming.

Talking and listening in multimodal contexts

Talking and listening occurred as students responded to print or digital texts they had read, viewed, listened to, wrote and produced. Talking and listening were not isolated skills as they usually involved students collaborating to investigate a topic and negotiating to construct a product for an audience to demonstrate their learning. Collaboration included networking and connecting to texts and each other in both a physical and virtual sense. Often students engaged in craft, art, music or drama activities within these processes. Thus further descriptors of talking and listening need to include aspects that represent more continuous communication such as collaborating, investigating, negotiating, enacting, connecting, interacting, and networking.

These additional descriptors of language and literacy practices are proposed based on evidence from the research detailed in this book. They explain how the modes of talking, listening, reading, viewing and writing have been extended and need to be reconsidered because of the way digital technology has changed social communication practices. Differences occur, not only in interaction between different modes in the processes of reading or writing on screen or online, but in the interaction between students.

Aspects that have not been considered in this study in relation to reading and writing in virtual environments are intertexuality, intratextuality and the evolution of hybrid texts. These aspects need to be considered in any further descriptions of reading and writing as they are influencing texts that are interchanged though the web, particularly within social networking environments. The influences of such social practices were emerging as significant considerations within the data.

CHALLENGES

There were many exciting and innovative outcomes throughout the research that provide evidence that teachers were planning creatively to engage students in effective literacy learning. There are however several challenges existing within this relatively new learning environment. We need to accept that there are unanswered questions within a time of transition for education as we continue to blend new with traditional approaches to learning and teaching.

With the development of the subject English for a National Curriculum in Australia there is already a tension between calls for 'back to basics' and new approaches in literacy education. Similarly there is always a tension between the requirements of national testing and creative pedagogy. These tensions need to be acknowledged and addressed. We have to ensure that within the inclusion of digital technologies basic aspects of reading, reading comprehension, writing, vocabulary development, grammar, spelling and punctuation are still explicitly taught. However we also need to be clear about those aspects that are now 'basic' for reading and writing with digital and multimedia texts. Teachers in this project assessed students' reading and production of multimodal texts in relation to existing syllabus outcomes but further development is needed for specific assessment criteria that will reflect changing practices.

It is a challenge to know how to assess reading with digital texts and whether we monitor the same reading behaviours that are monitored for reading print-based texts. Current reading assessment is linked to print-based texts. Students were reading text on screen as well as in books for most tasks. When asked, students commented that reading on screen is 'different' from reading a book for them. Despite ongoing world-wide research that confirms this difference, it is difficult to isolate specific criteria to assess these multisensory differences. For example, we have shown that a new descriptor of reading includes making hyperlinks, browsing and navigating different pathways within web links. It has yet to be determined whether assessment of these aspects will provide a profile of a student's reading and viewing on screen. Furthermore, teachers need to know how to assist students with strategies for reading digital texts and to ensure the development of different levels of reading comprehension. Critical reading, discrimination and evaluation of messages, particularly from media and digital texts, are essential skills of a literate person in our contemporary age of instant, global messaging.

Additional descriptors of language and literacy are proposed. These descriptors, which are in accord with other ongoing research, need to be considered for incorporation into curriculum documents. It is hoped that the National Curriculum will formalise the integration of digital communications technology within the subject of English as well as in other curriculum subjects. While a digital environment enables more creative use of group work, we need to ensure that we monitor the literacy proficiency of individuals in all areas. The creative possibilities of embedding images, sound and music into text production allowed for students, who do not usually succeed with print-based tasks, to demonstrate competence with these technologies. Some developments have been proposed by other researchers (Bearne, 2003) for methods to assess students' creation of multimodal texts and further work is needed in this area.

While students are motivated to learn with digital technology they need to be able to maintain a sustained, concentrated approach to reading as appropriate to the purpose. For effective literacy students need to experience the intensity and variety of different forms of texts, their structure and language. Some teachers expressed concern that while students were highly motivated to complete tasks with IWBs and other technology, they became bored and not engaged with reading print-based texts. For example, one teacher commented that, 'reading digital texts can be fast paced and requires students to think but many often 'click' before they think'. In some cases during observations, students chose not to read the information and demonstrated difficulty in sustained reading online. It is important for teachers to develop strategies for engaging students in the enjoyment and study of literature within the use of digital technologies along with the sustained, critical reading of all types of texts appropriate to the purpose.

Design has been shown to be an integral process with multimodal literacy. We need further investigation about how much students need to understand and deconstruct the design and language of a visual or digital text to understand its meaning and purpose. Similarly, we need to consider what teachers and students need to know about design to produce a visual or digital text for a particular audience. A further challenge is to consider how the use of design can be integrated with the teaching of the writing of text types and their specific structure, language and grammar.

These are some of the many challenges that exist within changing classroom environments. Our research has shown that challenges can be met effectively if we continue to consider ways of building students' literacy capacity within authentic learning environments.

SUMMARY

The research has shown that teachers can develop new ways of teaching to embed digital technology within their programs. This requires new ways of programming and assessment. This process can be a significant and rewarding process of professional learning for teachers. To adjust to the realities of changed modes of communication, classrooms need to change and additional descriptors of literacy need to be extended to encompass the nature of multimodal literacy. Further challenges exist for teaching and assessment along with the need for more explicit acknowledgment of changed literacy practices in national curriculum documents.

Conclusion

It is impossible to do justice in this one book to the immense range of programs that the fifty participating teachers implemented to engage students in literacy and learning within the research reported here. Nor is it the purpose of the book to present a guide on how to use technology in the classroom. Rather, detailed examples from the research are presented for evidence of classroom change that has already occurred and to provide ideas and reflections for teachers.

> **The findings support the position that new modes of communication require new literacy practices and new texts; and that contemporary definitions of literacy need to incorporate descriptions of students' use of digital communication. Moreover, the evidence from the research demonstrates that teachers can combine these new literacy practices and texts in meaningful, effective ways for students' literacy and learning.**

Reading and writing tasks occurred on paper as well as on screen. Frequently these aspects of literacy were interrelated as students researched information for a particular content area and then wrote and produced different types of print and digital texts, supported by graphics, photography, sound or animation. In several programs teachers used literature as a focus, ensuring students' response to literature was developed at both affective and cognitive levels while using digital media to extend responses and comprehension.

Reading and writing were given a purpose within learning tasks that required students to produce a multimodal text such as a digital narrative, video or claymation. Knowing that a specific audience would view their work encouraged students to be concerned with the design of their final product. Networking through the use of wikis and blogs extended the social parameters of the classroom allowing students to interact with staff, parents and students within the school, other schools, and even another country. Wikis and blogs were effective as online journals and allowed students to respond with comment and critique to the work of other writers. Additionally, images (photoblog), audio (podcasting), videos (vlogs) and links to other blogs or web pages were used as appropriate.

Discussion of the holistic nature of the teachers' programs has shown the essential role of collaboration between students for contemporary learning contexts, and thus the importance of extending students' oral language proficiency to suit the purpose of different tasks. Digital records of students' work extended the possibilities of formative assessment within the teaching/learning cycle.

The research has shown that teachers were engaged in curriculum change. Teachers' professional learning was enhanced by being researchers in their own classrooms, working in teams, having the support from the School Executive, building networks with other schools and having their professionalism acknowledged, particularly through presentations to colleagues. Most teachers have communicated their work to other staff in their school and several have presented at national literacy conferences. Thus there has been ongoing communication and sustainability from some of the changes made to teaching and assessment.

Challenges remain. It is important to ensure that such curriculum change is sustained in an effective way. Further research is needed to more explicitly describe reading and writing in digital environments and to disseminate this research so that teachers understand these descriptors clearly for both teaching and assessment. It is essential to balance such new research with the requirements of national, standardised testing and the forthcoming National Curriculum.

There are many aspects to celebrate from the outcomes of the research, despite the challenges. The most important outcome was that students were motivated and engaged in literacy and learning. This engagement was a result of teachers knowing the curriculum, understanding the needs of their students, and planning creatively and effectively to blend traditional with new modes of learning. New communications and information technologies will continue to captivate and to challenge their users. New technologies will continue to evolve before new curricula are developed. If learning is at the centre of these changing dynamics teachers and students will adapt. A rich understanding of the multimodal potentials of literacy has been developed within the combined research of the Catholic Education Office, Sydney and the Australian Catholic University. It is hoped that this understanding will enable educators and students to adapt to new communication in the future.

The research provides evidence that teachers can combine students' print-based literacy learning with digital communications technology. This outcome was achieved by a change in pedagogy as teachers recognised the need to adapt classroom communication to those digital communication practices that students access outside school and that will be significant in the future for their students.

In all of the classrooms it was apparent that significant literacy and learning were occurring for students within the programs. In every case observed, students were all engaged in investigation by reading, searching and responding to information in books or screen-based texts. Through their investigations they were gaining knowledge of the curriculum content of specific content areas, understanding concepts and problem solving. Students were engaged in literacy practices, displaying metacognition, and using the metalanguage of the content area as well as the language of digital technology. Students were benefiting from the extended focus of units of work and the multiple tasks developed within these units. Literacy was occurring as an integrated, multimodal process within different curriculum areas.

The facilities of different digital technologies are both requiring and allowing teachers and students to work in a different way from the past. This reality entails many challenges in relation to resourcing and competencies as well as for programming and assessment. At the same time, the opportunities for engaging students in meaningful literacy and learning experiences are boundless and cannot be ignored. The voices of students throughout the project showed that they were motivated to learn in response to teachers developing multimodal environments. It is fitting to conclude with the voices of students from a Year 6 class who were asked to reflect on the learning that occurred for them during the research:

COMMENTS
- Multimodal learning makes education a lot easier. I learnt how to make a web page through freeweb.com. I put a lot of effort into the webpage I created.
- Multimodal learning is good because everyone gets to participate and take part.
- Multimodal learning is fun. Children get more intrigued in education if it's fun. I was happier to go to school because we were learning about fun stuff.
- I have learned more on websites with my friend because she might know something that I don't know, so then she can tell how to do that then I have learned something new.

This student's comment is an insightful description of the changed nature of reading and writing:

You're not just reading...with reading you go and read...
or with writing...you write on your own...with the computer
you're reading and writing together at the same time...'

There are many challenges that exist within changing classroom environments. Our research has shown that challenges can be met effectively if we continue to consider ways of building students' literacy capacity within authentic learning environments. The facilities of new technologies offer the potential for dynamic literacy learning. However it is not the technology itself that will create a vibrant, engaging learning environment but the way teachers plan and structure the learning experiences with rich language, literature and literacy practices. The examples in this book have shown how many teachers have structured exciting and effective literacy in multimodal learning environments.

REFERENCES

Australian Government, Department of Education, Employment and Workplace Relations (DEEWR) (2008), *The Digital Education Revolution*. http://www.digitaleducationrevolution.gov.au/

Australian Curriculum, Assessment and Reporting Authority (ACARA), (2009-10). Draft Australian Curriculum for English. http://www.acara.edu.au/phase_1_-_the_australian_curriculum.html

Barbalet, M. (1991), *The Wolf*, illustrated by Jane Tanner. Australia: Viking, Penguin Books Australia Ltd.

Barton, D. (1994), *Literacy. An introduction to the ecology of written language*. Oxford: Blackwell Publishing.

Bearne, E. (2003). Rethinking Literacy: Communication, Representation and Text. *Reading Literacy and Language*, 37:3, 98–103.

Bearne, E., Clark, C., Johnson, A., Manford, P., Mottram, M. & Wolstencroft, H. With Anderson, R., Gamble, N. & Overall, L. (2007), 'Reading on Screen', Research undertaken by the United Kingdom Literacy Association with support from the Qualifications and Curriculum Authority January–June 2006.

Bearne, E. & Wolstencroft, H. (2007), *Visual Approaches to Teaching Writing. Multimodal Literacy 5-11*, London: Sage.

Carrington, V. (2005), 'New textual landscapes, information and early literacy', in Marsh, J. (ed.) *Popular Culture, New Media and Digital Literacy in Early Childhood*, London: Routledge-Farmer, pp. 13–27.

Coiro, J., Knobel, M., Lankshear, C., & Leu, D. (Eds) (2008), *Handbook of Research on New Literacies*, New York: Lawrence Erlbaum Associates.

Cope, B. & Kalantzis, M. (2000) (Eds) The New London Group, *Multiliteracies: Literacy Learning and the Design of Social Futures*, Melbourne: Macmillan.

Cummins, J. (1984), *Bilingualism and Special Education: Issues in Assessment and Pedagogy*. Great Britain: Multilingual Matters, Ltd.

Gee, J. (2003), Gee, J. (2003), *What Video Games have to Teach us about Learning and Literacy*. New York: Palgrave Macmillan.

Halliday, M.A.K. (1985), *Spoken and written language*. Victoria: Deakin University Press.

Hansford, D. & Adlington, R. (2009), 'Digital spaces and young people's online authoring: challenges for teachers', in *Australian Journal of Language and Literacy*, 32, 1: 55–68

Healy, A. (2008), 'Expanding Student Capacities' in Healy, A. (Ed.) *Multiliteracies: Pedagogies for diverse learners*. Sydney: Oxford University Press, pp.2–29.

Izhar, T. & C. (2006), *The Wolf's Story: What Really Happened to Little Red Riding Hood*, Walker Books:London.

Kalantzis & Cope, B. (2005), *Learning by Design*. http://l-byd.com/pics/LbyDOverviewDec04.pdf. Accessed 12 December 2007.

Kervin, L. (2009), 'Possibilitieis for Literacy Learning through Podcasting Activities.' *E:update* 005. Sydney: e:lit.

Kress, G. and van Leeuwen, T. (1996), *Reading Images. The Grammar of Visual Design*. London: Routledge.

Kress, G. and van Leeuwen, T. (2001), *Multimodal Discourse*, London: Routledge.

Kress, G. (2003), *Literacy in the New Media Age*. London: Routledge.

Kress, G. (2010). Multimodality. *A social semiotic approach to contemporary communication*. London: Routledge.

Kress, G. & Jewitt, C. (Eds.) (2003), *Multimodal Literacy*, New York: Peter Lang.

Lankshear, C. and Knobel, M. (2003). *New Literacies Changing Knowledge and Classroom Learning*. Buckingham: Open University Press.

Lawless, K.A. & Schrader, P.G. (2008), 'Where Do We Go Now? Understanding Research on Navigation in Complex Digital Environments', in Coiro, J., Knobel, M., Lankshear, C., & Leu, D. (Eds) (2008). *Handbook of Research on New Literacies*. New York: Lawrence Erlbaum Associates, PP.267-296.

Lewis, C. & Farbos, B. (2005), 'Instant messaging, literacies and social identities', *Reading Research Quarterly*. 40:4, 470–501.3.

Luke, A. & Freebody, P. (1999), 'Further notes on the four resources model' in *Reading Online*, http:/www.readingonline.org/research/lukefreebody.html.

Marsh, J. (2002), 'Popular culture, computer games and the primary literacy curriculum', in Monteith, M. (ed.) *Teaching Primary Literacy with ICT*. Buckingham: Open University Press, pp.127–143.

Marsh, J., Brooks, G., Hughes, J., Ritchie, L., Roberts, S., & Wright, K. (2005), 'Digital beginnings: Young children's use of popular culture, media and new technologies' Literacy Research Centre, University of Sheffield.

http://arrts.gtcni.org.uk/gtcni/bitstream/2428/27212/1/DigitalBeginningsReport.pdf

Nayar, N. and Roy, P. (2009), *What Shall I Make?* Tricycle Press: New York

Pahl, K. & Rowsell, J. (2005), *Literacy and Education. Understanding the New Literacy Studies in the Classroom*. London: Paul Chapman Publishing.

Prensky, M. (2001). Prensky, M. (2001), 'Digital Natives, Digital Immigrants', in Prensky, M., *On the Horizon* (MCB University Press, Vol. 9 No. 5, October 2001), http://www.marcprensky.com/writing/Prensky%20-%20Digital%20Natives,%20Digital%20Immigrants%20-%20Part1.pdf. Accessed 24 January 2009.

Ridell, C. (2008), *Wendel's Workshop*. Macmillan: London

Scieszka, J. & Smith, L. (1989), *The True Story of the Three Little Pigs by A. Wolf*. New York: Viking.

Simpson, A. (2004), 'Book Raps as online multimodal communication: towards a model of interactive pedagogy', *International Journal of Learning*, 10, 2705–2714.

Snyder, I. (ed.) (1997), *Page to Screen. Taking literacy into the electronic era*. Sydney: Allen & Unwin.

Street, B. (1995), *Social Literacies*. London: Longman.

Unsworth, L. (2001). *Teaching Multiliteracies Across the Curriculum. Changing contexts of text and image in classroom practice*, Buckingham: Open University Press.

Unsworth, L. (2003), 'Re-framing research and literacy relating to CD-ROM narratives: Addressing 'radical change' in digital age literature for children', *Issues in Educational Research*, 13(2), 55–70.

Wagner, J. (1997), 'The unavoidable intervention of educational research: A framework for reconsidering researcher-practitioner co-operation', *Educational Researcher*. 26 (7) 13–22.

Walsh, M. (2006), 'The "textual shift": examining the reading process with visual and multimodal texts', *Australian Journal of Language and Literacy*, 29:1, 24–37.

Walsh, M. (2008), 'Worlds Have Collided And Modes Have Merged: Classroom Evidence Of Changed Literacy Practices', in *Literacy*, 42:2, pp.101–108

Walsh, M. (2009). Chapter 3. In Pedagogic Potentials of Multimodal Literacy. In Tan Wee Hin, L & Subramanian, R. (Eds) *Handbook of Research on New Media Literacy at the K-12 Level: Issues and Challenges*. Volumes 1 and 11. US: IGI Global, pp. 32-47.

Walsh, M. (in press 2010), 'Multimodal literacy. What does it mean for classroom practice?' in *Australian Journal of Literacy*, October.

Yelland, N., Lee, L., O'Rourke, M., & Harrison, C. (2008), *Rethinking Learning in Early Childhood Education*, Berkshire, UK: Open University Press.

GLOSSARY

Animation, Claymation or 'stop animation': photographs of the movement of an object, one frame at a time, and the rapid combination of these in a movie to create a sense of movement. Claymation is when the clay figures are made to be photographed and animated.

Blog: or weblog, is a type of website for online communication usually maintained by an individual with regular entries. Blogs are interactive and can allow for visitors to enter, read or view material and leave comments via 'posts'.

Comiclife: software that can be used to create photo albums or comic strips incorporating the user's photographs and allowing control of layout and text.

Digital literacy: reading and writing with digital texts in a digital or virtual environment and includes the technical skills required to operate the computer or mobile device, and use icons or symbols to view and create digital texts.

Digital texts: texts viewed and read on the screen of a computer or a hand-held mobile digital device.

Flip camera: a hand-held video recorder approximately the same size as a mobile phone operated by a small number of buttons/touch screen with a USB attachment that can be inserted directly into a computer hard drive.

Garage Band: software that allows the user to create music or podcasts and edit sound or music in videos. http://www.apple.com/ilife/garageband/

HSIE: Human Society and its Environment, a Key Learning Area in the New South Wales primary school curriculum.

KLAs: Key Learning Areas or specific, essential curriculum subjects to be studied.

Interactive White Board (IWB): a screen that displays the desktop of a computer (often a laptop) on to a white display surface (white board) via a projector. The user can interact with the display using a finger, pen or pointer on the white board or the mouse and keyboard on the computer.

Medium: the means of communicating a message, e.g. paper, computer screen, phone screen, television, IWB, film, camera, musical instrument.

Mode: the way the message is communicated, e.g. through spoken or written language, image, sound, gesture, movement, time and space.

Movie maker: Windows Movie Maker 2.1 available for free download from the web is software that allows the user to edit their own movie files and share them via CD, email or the web.

Multiliteracies: the communicative strategies needed for new as well as traditional types of communication in different social and cultural contexts.

Multimodality: a study of the communicative process, particularly how meaning is communicated through different semiotic or meaning-making resources and in different social contexts.

Multimodal literacy: the simultaneous reading, processing and/or writing, designing, producing and interacting with various modes of print, image, movement, graphics, animation, sound, music and gesture

Multimodal texts: texts that have more than one mode, such as print and image or print, image, sound and movement and is often a digital text but can be a book, such as picture book, information text or graphic text requiring the processing of more than one mode.

Multimodal learning environments: classroom environments where teachers and students are using and interacting with different types of texts and tasks across a range of curriculum areas.

New Literacies: a term originally used to describe the way new technologies were creating new literacies and which now incorporates the social and cultural changes that have accompanied changed literacy and communication practices.

Ning: an online platform for the creation of social networking websites based on individual interests and incorporating individual design, layout, features and membership information.

Pedagogy: the practice and methods of teaching.

Podcasts & vodcasts: the online delivery of audio and video digital files to a mobile device such as an *ipod* or a *MP3* player.

Semiotics: how signs are used to convey meaning, particularly through different modes.

SOSE: Studies of Society and the Environment, a Key Learning Area in the Victorian primary school curriculum.

VoiceThread: a web based platform for group discussions. The network allows users to record audio files such as reading aloud or singing and attach accompanying movies, still images or documents.

Wiki: a website that allows for easy creation and editing of interlinked web pages. A range of visual and textual media can be included in a wiki. Wikis also contain features that allow for discussions to occur between users.

A more detailed version of this glossary may be found on the e:lit website:www.elit.edu.au